DCML
60

·Ɔ[*Western* [Ɔ·
GHOST TOWNS

BODIE BUTTE is now almost a hollow mountain because of old mine workings. In winter, freezing made a problem for burials in the cemetery, so miner's blasting powder was used to break the ground. It is said that during an early typhoid epidemic that the ominous booming from the graveyard was almost continuous.

Western GHOST TOWNS

BY

LAMBERT FLORIN

Maps and Drawings
by
DAVID C. MASON, M.D.

SUPERIOR PUBLISHING COMPANY - SEATTLE

WESTERN GHOST TOWNS

is dedicated to David C. Mason, M.D.,

whose help and encouragement

have made this book possible.

PHOTOGRAPHERS' CAMP at base of Mt. Whitney, crag at right of center. Keeler Needle is first spire at left of main peak. Mountain is backwall to immense glacial cirque, whose melt waters made important contribution to formation of Owens Lake.

INTRODUCTION

In the spring of 1955 Dr. David Mason of Beaverton, Oregon, and I were planning our vacation. It was to be devoted mainly to mountain climbing. This had been my usual pattern for a number of years and David was about to have his first try at roughing it. Our objectives were several—to fish for the fabulous Golden trout in the high country to the west of Mount Whitney, to study the effects of glacial action in that clean, uncluttered area, to find a rare primrose, Primula Suffrutescens, and to spend a night on the summit of Mt. Whitney at 14,495 feet.

We wrote ahead to the packer at Lone Pine, California, arranged for horses to take us into the mountain wilderness centered by Crabtree Meadows and waited with impatience for the middle of July.

Before we got away a copy of *Sunset* magazine arrived, and in it was a short article on Bodie, California. This was a Ghost Town near the Nevada border. There were a few pictures of the little Methodist Church and the old firehouse. The idea of a town, once teeming with life and action, now dead and deserted was intriguing, and we resolved that if time permitted, we would stop by and visit Bodie on our return.

Everything went according to plan, except for car trouble and nearly missing the pack-train as a consequence. We rode easily by horseback up the winding switchbacks to Muir Pass, over the knife-blade crest to suddenly face that staggering panorama of endless miles of snowy High Sierra peaks. Then sharply down, and at long last as evening approached we were abandoned in the meadow, in some of the most beautiful country in America.

Then came the fishing, the camping and a gradual move on foot higher and higher until we spent a night well above timberline at about 12,000 feet.

All around our camp grew thousands of the rose-pink primroses in full bloom, arranging themselves in garlands around the base of each huge granite boulder. All this was set in the center of a large glacial cirque, formed by a monster mass of ice long gone.

Next morning we pushed along the crest toward the summit of Mt. Whitney, each with a full load of equipment including several cameras.

We were forced to wait out a severe lightning and hailstorm, just short of the summit. Lightning on these high places can be especially dangerous, often taking the form of all-over discharges of energy from which there is no protection. After it was over, snow and hail made the crevices white, a pale sun came out for a while, and we then gained the summit.

As it grew dark we looked down at the Owens Valley town of Lone Pine some 11,000 feet below. Looking east and north we could see endless stretches of desert, valleys and mountains. Somewhere to the north would be Bodie, which we knew now, we would see in a couple of days.

The night was cold and comfortless, and dawn brought another storm, so down we went with almost no pictures. We reached our car toward evening in a deluge of rain. Next morning the sun bathed the summit of our mountain, too late!

We made the mistake of approaching Bodie from the road beginning at Mono Lake, not knowing that the alternate from near Bridgeport is much better, but even so we had no real difficulty.

We had been talking, but as we rounded a curve and saw the town we fell silent. Spread out before us were many buildings silent and empty, streets grown over with grass, yards filled with sagebrush. More than 12,000 people had once lived here; now no one.

We agreed later that for the time being at least, we had climbed our last mountain, that from now on we would devote our vacations to hunting the fascinating remnants of a bygone era, and to make the best pictorial records of them we could.

The towns photographed so far are only the beginning, but they represent a cross section of the camps in the West. We have none from the Mother Lode country in California, feeling that this area should be treated separately and completely, its history being so much more homogenous. We have a goodly group from nine states, none at all from Utah and New Mexico. Some of these gaps will be closed, we hope, in a future volume.

There are many "fringe benefits" separate from but directly related to search for an abandoned town. Some of these joys are somewhat questionable at the time,

7

better in retrospect. On the approach to St. Elmo, Colorado, the road had been quite good. While steep and narrow, it had a good gravel surface well above the level of the torrent foaming alongside. But then it dropped to the level of the stream, which at this point took over, covering the road with a foot or so of churning water and gravel. There had been a thunderstorm in the higher mountains the night before, and we were marooned. About this time, from the upper stretches of dry road, a grader arrived, and with its huge blade pushed a wall of gravel aside, diverting the flood and allowing us to proceed. On our return, the stream had shrunk to its normal size and retreated from the road.

The road to Animas Forks, Colorado, tamely follows the precipitous gorge of the Animas River from Silverton to a point just above Eureka. Then it narrows, of necessity, and plunges wildly upward along the rocky side of a cliff, on a ledge blasted out of the verticle wall. The grade isn't too bad, since it once served the narrow gauge railroad, but it is often filled with loose rocks. These have fallen by simple gravity, or sheep scrambling up the banks have dislodged them. One walks ahead of the car, rolling boulders into the canyon below.

The dirt road to Greenhorn, Oregon, is a poor to fair one in dry weather except for dust, but after fall rains it develops small bogs in spots covered with water for an unknown depth. After the "front man" has removed his shoes and socks and wades through several of these, he finds the bottom quite firm and waves the driver on, then gets back in the car with feet well chilled.

The route to Fairview, Nevada, is a good example of a gravel and dirt road not bad on the level, but sometimes deeply rutted on the grades where violent deluges from the mountains have carved random gullies. Many desert side roads may be quite solid except where they cross a dry wash. Here the car may settle down, to rest on its belly on the sand. Major excavation becomes necessary, or the wheels may be jacked up and a firmer footing of rocks or brush placed under them. Desert-wise ghost-town hunters will get out of a wash as fast as possible in threatening weather since a wall of water may come sweeping down its natural course. The same possibility precludes selecting a camp site in a wash or canyon floor, however attractive the spot may be.

Camping is to many a joy in itself, and to the traveler who is interested in the best light for pictures, a camper's independence is a boon. Arrival time at his town may be just before nightfall with the light all wrong or gone. Next morning means a reversal of illumination.

Our entry to Elkhorn, Montana, was spectacular, heralded by fanfare of crackling thunder and a deluge of rain. Impatience called for a tour of the place anyhow. The clouds parted, allowed a low, red sun to bathe the old walls with a warm glow, beautiful, but useless for photography, being too transitory. We drove to a spot on the stream just below town where a grove of aspen trees stood, their white trunks gleaming in the failing light. Next morning a brilliant sun shone on this gem among old towns. We felt the possibilities warranted spending the full day, watching the light change and taking advantage of it for our pictures. Anticlimax next morning was a start of only a half mile when a flat tire showed a hand-forged nail, buried to its square head! It is wrong to carry away souvenirs and we can only hope we may be excused for this particular theft.

On the 1960 trip we found we couldn't make the steep grade to Cerro Gordo, California, with our load of camping gear and rocks, so we backed down, crossed the

Owens Valley (once a huge lake) and made camp at the foot of Mt. Whitney. Unloading everything, we spent the night there beside Lone Pine Creek, and next morning with our car empty except for camera equipment easily went up that spectacular grade, once traversed only by mule teams.

The next two days were spent making another climb of Mt. Whitney, under more favorable weather conditions than before. A sudden windstorm in our absence blew over the tent, upsetting the water-can. Since the tent doesn't leak *out* either, everything inside was well soaked.

A camp south of Battle Mountain, Nevada, was made on the dump of an old turquoise mine. A diligent search of this rock pile before dark rewarded us with several chunks of turquoise matrix, to be cut and polished next winter. As soon as it was dark enough, I got out the short-wave ultraviolet lamp and went over the ground for fluorescent rocks. A foot or so from my sleeping bag I surprised a scorpion, who in turn surprised me by fluorescing a bright chartreuse color.

At Rochester, Nevada, night wasn't far off and below town we found a beautifully level spot of sand and gravel, drove into the middle of it and got out to make camp. I was startled by a yell and a pointed finger. David had discovered the site's rightful tenant, a large rattlesnake. Our council of war was over almost before it started, the rattler had been there first; the least we could do, we felt, was to allow him his privacy. We found another spot less level, but unoccupied!

The night was freezing in the Blue Mountains near Bonanza, Oregon, and we had put up the umbrella tent. Toward midnight there was a chorus of coyote howling from many points. Then came that indescribably eerie wail from just outside the tent. My little dog started out to drive the intruder off, but I felt the battle would be an unequal one, and held her back.

Other intimate animal and bird contacts have been numerous on our searchings, a magnificent Golden Eagle alighting on a snag nearby, a coyote by daylight surprisingly large and wolf-like, a deer daintily walking through camp in the evening while we held our breaths, horned toads, caught in the desert, who would sit trustingly on one's hand, blinking jewel-like eyes, small versions of some prehistoric dinosaur.

These reptiles, animals and birds, the plants and trees, the rocks and minerals, minor accidents and adventures have added up to increased enjoyment of the trips made in search of ghost towns.

Many patterns become apparent as we go along, perhaps the plainest and most important is that the surface of the road means everything to the condition of the town. An old mining camp directly on a paved highway is never completely deserted; at the very least there will be a filling station, a tavern or tiny store. At most it will become a famous tourist attraction, as is Virginia City, either the one in Nevada or in Montana. This is good or bad according to the personal feelings involved.

Our own way of thinking is that *any* addition or change detracts from the undeniable charm of the unspoiled original. Granted, a new roof and repairs contribute toward prolonging the life of an old structure ready to collapse. The trouble is, such "improvements" seldom take into account the character and charm of the original. Exceptions to this are plentiful in Virginia City, Montana. Here it is almost impossible to discern the additions and protective repairs.

Perhaps our viewpoint is completely selfish, but we want our ghost town to appear as if we were the first to enter the town in many years! And to get to this kind of town, you almost always have to walk the last few miles, or have handy a four-wheel drive rig. We've never minded walking and are well equipped with stout boots, pack sacks, sleeping bags and, most important of all, a thermos bottle full of hot coffee! By the time the pack sack has also received its quota of cameras, lenses and equipment it gets pretty heavy, but weight is forgotten with the first sign of a weathered, sagging little structure. Such a one on the outskirts of our objective will almost invariably be a cabin beside a small mine shaft or tunnel. If in the high mountains such as in the San Juans of Colorado, the little structure is likely to be precariously clinging to a cliff and over-hanging a raging torrent of melting snow water. Banks of snow will still be whitening the shady sides of the banks, blue columbines dancing on the sunny ones. If our little shanty is in the blazing desert of Arizona or Nevada it will be surrounded by sagebrush, and if early enough in the year, there will be ocotillos in bloom, waving their scarlet racemes overhead, with sand verbenas for a rose colored carpet.

Shortly after passing this outpost we see another and another. Each will be be-side a sprawled out pile of rocks, fanning out from the mouth of the mine. This is the "dump," the waste material cast aside as worthless. The dump will always be of a dif-ferent color from the more weathered surface rock, often conspicuously so, making a scar on the hillside, vividly white, cream or red.

About the same time we have been noticing other piles of rocks, not rough, blasted ones, but smooth, waterworn cobblestones in the stream bed. These are oddly regular in an irregular sort of way, like waves in the sea. They are the digested material dis-gorged by the dredges which have been gobbling up the stream beds and extracting the gold therefrom.

The dumps are now more numerous and more buildings appear; some are larger and there will be houses, mostly single dwellings. A big mill and its adjoining tailings dump has been blocking our view, but we walk around this, and there is our objective, our ghost town.

We are looking down the dirt street, once so teeming with life. The thoroughfare is now completely deserted, filled with grass and sagebrush, a few sun-purpled bottles lie scattered about. Enough buildings still line the street to give form to the town. Some are hotels, theaters, stores with a large proportion of saloons. Many have false fronts, the most characteristic feature of the architecture of the times when they were built. On these will be faintly discernible the signs advertising what went on inside, their colors muted, or all but gone.

In one case the front door has been closed and bolted, but rust has long since taken the fastenings and the door hangs askew. A huge clump of sagebrush has grown in the entrance, but squeezing by this aromatic barricade we find ourselves in gloom made more intense by the glare outside. Details emerge, a long counter along one side shows where colossal thirsts were assuaged. Small round tables and broken chairs are scattered and overturned on the bare plank floor. Wallpaper imported from England and elegant in its day, hangs in tattered fragments from the walls. As a breeze comes through the empty windows these streamers sway with ghostly grace, or flap wildly in stronger winds.

At the side a flight of steps leads upstairs. At one time entrance was more pri-vately gained behind a filigreed screen but this has fallen and shattered. We try the step gingerly, for safety, and gain the upper floor. Here a short hall divides two rows of rooms, each furnished with a brass bedstead and a little stand. Here were ensconced the "girls" who advertised their wares on the dance floor below.

Pack rats by the dozen live here now. They have covered the planks with an inch of droppings, and have long since confiscated the stuffing of mattresses for their nests.

Down we go to emerge at the back door. Here, attached to the building is the "little house out back." The rims of the holes in the seats have been chewed by porcupines.

The yard at the rear of the saloon is filled with a welter of rubbish of another day. Old wagon wheels seem to predominate, along with piles of bottles and other debris. All this is overgrown, unsightly outlines mantled by a growth of vines and brush.

Next door to our saloon stood the church, apparently a large one, so extensive are the foundations. No walls or ceilings remain, only lines of rotting boards. Where the altar once stood, a carved wooden cross lies rotting in the grass. Good-sized trees, juniper and pinon pine, grow where the altar rail once was. Pew ends, also carved, faintly mark the aisle.

Next comes an almost perfectly preserved building, made of stone salvaged from the mine dumps. Windows and front doors, tall and narrow, are covered by heavy iron shutters, protection against bandits and thieves. This was the office of the Pony Express.

The bank itself came next, after a vacant space, but has been lost in one of the frequent fires plaguing the old towns. Now only a red brick vault remains. It has iron doors also, but these have sagged, allowing all sorts of old telegrams and checks cancelled in 1885 to scatter in the wind.

A firehouse stands a block away, topped by a tiny belfry. Sheltered inside are two hose carts, each surmounted by a little bell on a coiled spring. Rotting canvas hose is still rolled on the reel. Proud equipment, but inadequate to save the bank, for there was not enough water pressure and the volunteer firemen were drunk.

A tiny post office across the street has no roof; the sliding window, through which mail was passed has no glass. Sagebrush grows inside, a hop vine persists on the front.

The building next door seems to have been a store, but it leans so crazily to one side that we are satisfied with a peek through a window. There are shelves lining the walls, a counter across the front, a heavy pall of dust lies over everything.

No matter what the design, architecture or relative state of repairs, all the buildings have one conspicuous feature in common. This is the beauty of weathered wood or stone. The gray of fir and spruce, red of pine and redwood can only be attained by many years of rain and sun. Grain is enhanced by the passing years and in desert towns has often been sandblasted, bringing out detail in sharp relief.

At the edge of town lies the cemetery. Here the older graves have been marked by a rounded headboard of wood. The painted inscription is nearly unreadable but on one a favorable sidelight reveals the letters raised by weathering of the unpainted portion. More affluent occupants have their resting places enclosed by a fence often elaborately carved, or made of wrought iron.

It is late in the day now, long shadows stretch across the main street. Night will soon come to our little town, but there will be no one to light the kerosene lamp that hangs on the wall of the little cabin we pass on the way down to another world.

WHAT IS A GHOST TOWN?

One of several dictionary definitions of "ghost" is "a shadowy semblance of its former self." We have elected to prefer this somewhat ambiguous phrase, because it accurately describes many towns on the borderline of being dead or alive. Most of the towns described and pictured in this book are "dead" ghosts, but some still have life, though nothing to compare with the lusty vigor they enjoyed in their heyday.

Some even have a future, and the shadowy remnants of a fascinating past are being sacrificed on the altar of a new strike, possibly of a newer metal such as Molybdenum. An example of this is Kokomo, Colorado. Here is a town full of interesting relics of Colorado's early mining days with a corner full of new buildings and developments.

Some have never really died but are much smaller than before, with a population sufficient to keep up a post office, a store or two and an eating place (and, of course, a tavern). Examples a r e Skamokawa, Washington; Shaniko, Oregon and Gem, Idaho. Many others still have a community spirit and hopes for a brighter future, perhaps more brilliant than the past.

Some are even crowded with people. The saloons are "revived," some buildings "restored" and in general are inflated with a sort of artificial respiration. Examples are Virginia City, Nevada and the town with the same name in Montana. These are well worth while, easily accessible and full of diversion, but they lack the charm of the deserted or nearly deserted places, for some, at least.

Our ideal is a town completely abandoned by all business and permanent residents, and many of the subjects included fall into this category.

GHOST TOWN ETIQUETTE

Such souvenirs as are found in the brush by the side of the road are legitimately carried home. Parts of buildings still standing, or furniture in them, we don't include in the souvenir category, however. The old towns are melting away too fast as it is.

One of the towns in our book, Shaniko, Oregon was written up in a local newspaper this year, and about the same time was a subject for a T. V. program. The results to the town were drastic. One of the tiny group of remaining inhabitants wrote to the newspaper as follows—"Today, your cameraman would find something new added to the panorama he viewed a few weeks ago," reads the letter. "The inhabitants have been forced to tack up 'No trespassing' signs, in order to preserve a bit of privacy and rights as property owners. Why? Because the public is carrying Shaniko away, piece by piece. . . . Among us are several who have had belongings of varied value, both sentimental and intrinsic, taken from their property, and the schoolhouse and surroundings have been devastated by souvenir-seekers. In short, our privacy has been invaded and we are irked to say the least . . ."

ACKNOWLEDGMENTS

Six years and 25,000 miles after the first visit to Bodie, the collection of pictures has become a book. My hope is that those who plan to visit the towns we have recorded so far will have some idea what to expect and that perhaps even more readers in the category of armchair travelers may, in imagination, enjoy a visit to these reminders of an era vanishing from the American scene.

I hold a full-time job as florist designer, so that time for taking the pictures, doing interviews and research has been limited to an annual two-week vacation, plus a few three-day weekends.

This means that in order to augment information for the stories and captions I have had to rely rather heavily on periodicals and books already in print. I wish here to acknowledge my thanks and deep appreciation to the authors and publishers. Periodicals referred to are *Sunset, Desert, Arizona Highways* and the *Mineralogist.* Among the books are two top-ranking volumes on the subject. The first one, bought after Bodie, was *The Bonanza Trail* by the "First Lady of Mining Camp Lore," Mrs. Muriel Sibell Wolle. The next was *Ghosts of the Glory Trail* by an intrepid lady who spends much time traveling in a camper-car, Nell Murbarger. Then followed the books produced as a writer's project during W.P.A. days by several publishing houses; these include *Washington, Oregon* and *Nevada* by Binfords and Mort, Portland, Oregon; *Arizona, Montana, California* and *Colorado* by Hastings House, New York, N. Y.; *Idaho* and *Wyoming* by Oxford Press, New York, N. Y. Each state included is described in great detail. Unfortunately times have changed since then and many towns described in these guides as "well preserved" have vanished entirely, except for foundations. But their history remains unchanged.

Here They Dug the Gold by George F. Willison is invaluable to the student of Colorado history, and Leadville in particular. Another book called simply *Colorado*, by Frank Fossett, published in 1880 is not only quaint but full of the flavor of the day, all of it optimistic. Those busy mining towns would prosper forever! Two books must now be added to the list; they are, *Gemstones of America* by John Sinkankas and *Oregon Geographic Names* by Lewis A. McArthur. A booklet called *The Story of Keeler* by Frances Krautter also gives much data on Cerro Gordo, and another, *The Photo Story of the Matchless Mine and Baby Doe Tabor* by Caroline Bancroft is loaded with facts of that grandiose and tragic story.

Mrs. Ella Cain of Bridgeport, California, helped not only with Bodie but Masonic, California, with her books, *The Story of Early Mono* and the *Story of Bodie.*

Of individuals who have helped me, the list is endless. Perhaps the first of these should be my typist, Mrs. Dorothea Lloyd. She has untangled my almost illegible longhand, patiently, as far as I know, and with the interest in the subject necessary to stay with the task.

People who have generously given of their time for interviews in person and endless long-distance telephone conversations are mentioned in the text. Three of these I telephoned after the stories were completed. They are Mrs. Scott of Oatman, Arizona, Mr. Sabin Gray of the Ranch House Motel in Yerrington, Nevada and Mr. Robert Richards who is with the newspaper *Enterprise* of Virginia City, Nevada. These gave information needed to provide authentic captions for some of the pictures.

PHOTOGRAPHY

"Just looking" is enough for some. Prowling through the old buildings and trying to make out faded inscriptions on sagging headboards in the sage-grown cemetery is certainly fascinating. Good pictures to bring home for later study and to share with others will add much to the value of the vacation trip to the old, abandoned mining camp high on the mountain or out in the desert canyon.

There is a regrettable but growing tendency on the part of the amateur photographer to raise his 35mm camera to his eye, shoot, and let it go at that. This will provide many good records. Better quality and more interesting angles will result from the use of a tripod, especially if there is elasticity of imagination so that the camera is placed near the ground for one picture and perhaps high up in a second story window for the next.

Color transparencies are wonderful for showing to groups, but for a picture you can hold in your hands or make into a big print for the wall, black-and-white film should be exposed at the same time. Going over the same ground a second time with the other camera proves to be an anticlimax, or your light may be gone.

For black-and-white photography a fairly deep filter such as a G or even an A is almost indispensable for clouds and the beautiful texture in reddish, weathered boards.

For both cameras telephoto lenses do wonders for keeping buildings straight and for otherwise impossible groupings.

If you are camping, you will have the advantage of waiting overnight for the first light to be on the other side of the street, or for a stormy sky to clear off. Lighting and texture are everything and are tied together. The same wall, flat and uninteresting in a head-on light, will be intricately textured when illuminated from the side.

Most of the black-and-white pictures reproduced in this book were made with a Rolleiflex, and 90 percent of them with a filter. A few which seemed to require a telephoto lens were done with the Soligor, that camera having interchangeable lenses. Only rarely have I hand held the camera, and almost always have regretted such haste. Such pictures can always be detected by their lack of sharp detail.

The color pictures were all made with an Exacta 35mm. Many of these were taken through various lengths of telephotos from 135mm to 600mm.

More color was made hand held, to eliminate lugging two tripods and because the greater depth of field allowed large apertures and consequently faster exposures.

A WAIT OF HALF AN HOUR brought sun around to lend relief, making lettering stand out boldly. Cemetery in St. Louis, Oregon. This was a mission town settled by Catholic priests.

HEADBOARD stands in shadow of gallows, at Bannack, Montana.

TABLE OF CONTENTS

SKAMOKAWA, WASHINGTON

Until the year 1915 the town of Skamokawa had no land connection with the outside world. Surrounded on three sides by rocky cliffs and dense virgin timber, on the fourth by the broad lower Columbia River, the inhabitants took to the water.

Situated in Wahkiakum County in the state of Washington, Skamokawa is less than 80 miles northwest of Vancouver, yet is unknown to many Portlanders. It will repay the one-day tripper with its blend of Ghost Town atmosphere and live fishing and farming community.

It would be hard to say exactly when the town got started. Since there have been Indians, there has been some sort of village there, made up of fairly permanent aborigines. Fishing then, as now, has always been good along the lower river, the most desired fish being the Chinook Salmon, because of its delicately flavored red meat. The earliest whites found the peaceable Chinook Indians catching their staple food in the most primitive of nets and weirs, made of willow stems bound together with twine of twisted cedar-bark fibers.

Shortly after the Hudson's Bay Post was established at Fort Vancouver in 1825, other posts were strung along strategic routes. One of these was less than three miles from Skamokawa. A labyrinth of waterways, sloughs and creeks intersect the area. A peculiarity of the waterways funnels fog into the place, causing the Indians to give it the name, meaning "Smoke-on-the-water." (Pronunciation is Ska-mo'ka-wuh.)

The natives built up a steady trade in supplying the new Hudson's Bay Post with fish. Up until then they had always dried their catch (a dubious accomplishment in this damp atmosphere), ground the result into powder and stored it for the winter. A deerskin full of this stuff must have been a hard thing to live with, especially if the shelter grew warm and the air close. But now the post introduced the method of salting down, an only slightly less odoriferous method of preservation. The casks full of fish were sent up the river to Fort Vancouver, from whence they were shipped to England.

All went well until one day the Factor was found murdered and everything of value at the post stolen. Soldiers were sent down from Fort Vancouver to deal with the culprit, who, it was naturally assumed, would be found among the Chinooks. But these people were not given to deeds of violence, and were outraged. In effect, they said, "We didn't do it, but we know who did, and we'll bring him in" and they did, too.

Some time previously, a ship had been wrecked on the shores of the Olympic Peninsula, to the north. The crew had chosen a bad spot to be shipwrecked, because here lived the savage Hoh Indians. The entire crew was slaughtered, the ship pillaged. It was a member of this rapacious tribe who had wandered south and committed the crime at the post. He didn't enjoy his ill-gotten gains long; the indignant Chinooks, eager to prove their innocence, tracked the luckless Hoh down and returned him to their village. On the spot where one day the present schoolhouse would be built, he was tried and summarily hung. The noose had been knotted before the trial was finished. This headlong rush of justice was in striking contrast to later laxity among white settlers on the site.

Mr. L. E. "Les" Silverman, who was born in Skamokawa in 1897 and lives there still, provides much information.

When Mr. Silverman's father, C. L., arrived there in the 80's, there was quite a little town along the inner waterway called Skamokawa Creek. The creek is submerged in tidal water backed up from the river and is actually more like a canal. Along this waterway for perhaps a quarter mile stood a line of small buildings on each side. One side held most of the business structures; at least two of which, a saloon and a meat market, still stand precariously. In those days elk steak "tender and juicy" sold for eight cents a pound. The saloon, soon eclipsed by a fancier one, became the office of a tiny steamboat company called "Bobbidge & Holt." The name along with the words "Steamer Efin" are still faintly discernible on the front of the little building. The

FALSE FRONTS line this watery "Street." Many of the buildings are the original ones included in a painting of this scene made by T. S. Weedell, along in the 1880's.

name *Efin* was made up of the initial letters from the given names of the owning family. These were Edmond, Fred, Ida and Nellie.

All these structures faced the water, their rears the wilderness.

No man was ever tried for murder in Skamokawa since Indian days. This was in spite of not a few killings. One man, standing on the dock, whipped out his pistol and shot to death a man approaching in a boat. Presumably there had been bad blood between the two. The killer fled to the county seat, Cathlamet, gave himself up to the Sheriff, who turned him over to the Justice of the Peace. That worthy extracted 500 dollars from him as bail and pointedly suggested that he fade away for a while. He did so, moving to the Oregon side of the river. Every few weeks he came back to town on the early boat, visited his relatives and departed next day. He was never molested.

Skamokawa reached its peak in the first years of this century. About 1910 there were about 400 to 500 people, a fine schoolhouse had been built and three large shingle mills operated full tilt. The first co-operative creamery in the state was operating. A

PICTURESQUE HOTEL stood partly on wharf, partly on bank: was home to travelers who came to Skamokawa by river steamer. In times of high water in spring when snow in upper reaches of Columbia melted, hotel and wharf were surrounded by flood.

TIDAL EFFECTS ON LOWER Columbia are strong, as are fluctuations in seasonal levels of water. Walks on hinged connections and floating docks keep fishing boats accessible. Vat in foreground holds "blue vitrol" cupric compound in which nets are soaked, killing algae which would rot twine. Note roller, over which long gill net is fed into tank.

newer section had sprung up closer to the river itself. New docks, an imposing store and a three-story hotel faced the water. To them came, several times daily, the steamboats of the day. Sidewheelers and sternwheelers they were; the *Lurline*, the *Harvest Queen*, the *T. J. Potter* and all the rest.

But when river traffic died, so did something in Skamokawa. The big hotel emptied and faded, the store windows now stare on a sagging dock, the planks of which are rotting away and returning to the river. Empty, gray and weathered residences line a once busy steamboat slough, and the old school is forlornly a meeting place for the Redmen Lodge.

Mr. Silverman hopefully maintains the town is not dead and it never will become a true Ghost Town because there are still the fish and the fertile farmlands. Many docks are still draped with drying gill nets. Fish boats still ply the canals of once busy "Little Venice." A modern school stands at the edge of town where the guilty Hoh once swung at the end of a rope.

ONE OF THE ORIGINAL BUILDINGS, this was the Allison Brooks saloon, dates from 1888. Later became "Bobbidge & Holt Steamer Efin" office. Structure is no longer used, but gill nets are strung out on racks for drying and mending.

COPPER CITY, WASHINGTON

Mr. Fred Eaton has lived in the area of Copper City for nearly fifty years, and the town was already old and abandoned when he came. There had been a good strike of gold and copper, creating great but short-lived excitement. The great "Yacolt Burn," an enormous forest fire in 1902, stopped everything for a time and the mine was never worked profitably again. Mr. Eaton surmised that the vein had run out.

Some years later, a Sam Pumpelly conceived a plan to revilatize the mine and sell stock. "Sam drank a lot and would do anything to make a fast buck." He hauled good, rich ore from another mine and scattered it all over the diggin's. But his reputation was his undoing and the scheme fell through. He died not long after. Since then, the mine has been completely abandoned except for a few fishermen who cast their flies on the tumbling waters of Copper Creek.

LITTLE GROUP OF CABINS is swamped in rain-nurtured verdure.

INDEX, WASHINGTON

Index still has a few interesting buildings remaining from its lusty boom days, but they are fast disappearing. The most impressive still standing is the Fraternal Hall. The Red Men, the Masons and the Odd Fellows, tend to hold dear the old Hall.

The town is spectacularly situated, in what the pioneers called a "Hole." Surrounded by towering peaks in a wild section of the Cascades, it is bounded further by the rushing Skykomish River. Mt. Index with its pointing rock needles dominates as high a horizon as a town could have, and deep timber crowds close.

The post office was established in 1891, at which time the town was well underway and several mines were taking out a high grade copper ore called Bornite.

Amos Gunn's saloon was one of the largest during the town's boom days, but by no means the only one. Several more faced the main street running parallel to the river. Growth was slow until about 1897, when new veins were opened and the Sunset Copper Mine was being operated at such pressure that many men were killed in its tunnels and shafts. Hotels, drugstores, a newspaper and more saloons were established. Many more minerals were found, some only in traces, gold, silver, antimony, arsenates and even the "modern" molybdenum. When the copper deposits wore thin and attempts to exploit some of the others failed, the town died.

There are lots of open spaces now from which one can gaze up at the encircling peaks.

STEEP, TIMBERED SLOPES crowded old Index. Much virgin timber was cut for mine use, second growth was killed by fire. Now new growth is taking hold; in twenty years new forest will cover naked hills.

EARLY DAY FALSE FRONTS built during boom days looked down on wild mining and railroad construction camp.

SULTAN, WASHINGTON

Sultan, as were many Washington towns in the heavily timbered Cascades, was a combination mining and lumbering town. Some industry still persists, but the place doesn't begin to enjoy the color of the early days.

Sultan is now about as accessible as a town could be, barely off the highway. But in 1870 when prospectors found scattered flakes and a few nuggets of gold in the Sultan River, no roads existed, and timber as heavy as anywhere in the world covered the area. Indian trails made their way through the woods, and beside one of these John Nailor and his Indian wife established a claim ten years after the first discoveries.

Their place became a rough and tough hangout for all sorts of undesirables, thus setting the tone of Sultan's earlier days.

Prosperity was well established when the first light-draft river steamer, the *Mama*, reached the place in 1888.

Sultan really boomed when the Great Northern built its tracks on through the Cascades, one of the most staggering jobs in railroad history, and a separate story. The effect on Sultan, however, because of basing the men and materials there, was to expand an already rowdy mining camp into a sprawling mass of shacks housing all the hangers-on of a construction camp.

Sultan now is a quiet, respectable town. The buildings remaining from that wild, early period are on a back street.

TRINITY, WASHINGTON

Trinity is situated on Phelps Creek, in a wild, remote section of the Cascades. Heavy virgin timber crowds close.

Before the turn of the century there was prospecting, then placering nearby. Later, a rich vein of copper was found about five miles from the present site, and the first mine sank a shaft into the side of the mountain about 1900.

About 1914 the Royal Development Co. was formed and the town was built. A power plant was erected near the upper end of the main street. Large frame buildings followed; a mess hall, commissary, rooming houses and all the other structures necessary to a booming mining camp took shape. Another lesser street ran at right angles, fringed with smaller houses and cabins for the married men and their families. Above the power plant was the large mine building with the usual huge pile of tailings extending from it. On the older section of the latter was built a sawmill. Narrow gauge tracks led everywhere, and the dump ore cars ran back and forth between the openings of the shafts and tunnels and the mill.

Copper was the mainstay, although enough silver showed to pay actual cost of mining, 80 cents to the ton of ore. As costs increased and returns did not, operations began to slow down. There had been about 275 men working in the mines and the mill, but the number dwindled until at last everything stopped and everybody moved away, except one old man, a Mr. Foster, who stayed as watchman. Now even he is gone and the buildings stand silent and deserted. Many are crushed to the ground by the weight of winter snows totaling 30 feet some years. Dump cars are rusting on little rails, which look as if they were made for a long-gone toy engine. The skeleton of a deer lies inside the mill where the animal must have taken shelter in a winter storm and starved to death. The stream rushes through town, taking first one path and then another as the flushes of melting snows in spring urge it on.

OLD ORE CARTS stand rusting near mill.

OLD CABLE SPOOL reveals details in cross lighting.

THESE WERE MESS HALLS and dormitories for single miners. Structure at right has been crushed by weight of snow.

SPECTACULAR PEAKS of some of wildest parts of Cascades rise behind remains of Trinity as backdrop. Dense timber covers hills. Fuel and lumber were never problem here.

BLEWETT PASS, WASHINGTON

Blewett Pass in Washington was not so much a town as a continuous string of little towns, mines, mills and settlements, now faded away. There are many visible traces and in some cases a substantial reminder of those roaring days when thousand-dollar gold nuggets were not uncommon.

The most impressive of these is the Blewett Stamp Mill, north of the summit of the Pass. While much of the building is collapsed, enough stands to give a pretty good idea of what it once was.

An old gentleman lives in a tiny cabin across the road, his name is Anton Newbauer. Although the mill is completely useless now, he loves it still, having worked there as a young man. "You would never guess to look at the old mill now that there were hundreds of men working here in the 80's. Gold was what we mined here, and the lode was rich. There is still a lot of it down in that shaft and the tunnels that go clear back into the mountain. But the main vein pinched out about 1905, and the mill hasn't operated since. Now and then someone gets the idea of mining here again, but gold would have to be worth $200.00 an ounce to make it pay now."

Old Anton's estimate of a profitable price is far too high, according to later talks with other old hard-rock miners, but most are agreed on from $75.00 to $100.00. Everything depends on how much labor and machinery is needed for the amout of the yellow metal extracted. Simple, inexpensive placering operations are still paying off even at the present low price.

ORE LOADING chute is almost buried in rank vegetation typical of mountainous area. Even so, rainfall is much lighter on this east-facing side of Cascades. Timbers and logs would long since have rotted away on western rainy side.

OLD BLEWETT STAMP MILL reduced large chunks of rich gold ore into more manageable size for extraction. Weight was hauled to top of t o w e r (right), allowed to fall with crushing force on ore.

LIBERTY, WASHINGTON

The reason for a lively town's becoming of ghost status, in the case of Liberty, is quite simple. When news of big strikes in the Yukon reached camp, the entire population left for those greener pastures.

There were later gasps of life for a brief time. Some who had failed in Alaska came back and worked the creek bed for a time, but eventually left entirely. There was a brief revival in the 30's, but that too failed to bring any real stimulus to the dying town and at last it lay peacefully back to slumber in winter snows and summer sun.

Next to the school stood the only dance hall for many miles and people gathered "even from Montana" for the big dance of the year which was held at the opening of the deer season. Mostly, the dance deteriorated into brawls and fights. The lady who kept store across the street "used to come over and raise hell because she couldn't sleep." This went on for years, but she never got used to it.

Liberty is so high and so cool, while the nearby lowlands of eastern Washington are roasting, that several people take refuge in its old cabins during the summer. But this doesn't spoil its charm, or status as a bona fide Ghost Town. No business is transacted there, no children go to its old school and no gas is sold from the broken old pump which in the latest days of Liberty's existence served the Model T's.

The gravels of Swauk Creek are still worth $1.00 a yard, even at the present price of gold, but costs are too high to work them.

LIBERTY'S QUIET Main Street. School is at far end.

WILKESON, WASHINGTON

Here is a coal mining town that turned to lumbering, then to sandstone quarrying. This last still goes on to some extent, but the place has become a near Ghost Town with rows of sagging buildings lining the main street. Rusting unused railroad tracks run down the center, and brush and blackberry vines encroach on the sidewalks.

There are interesting old coke ovens, overgrown and not too easily found. These are the remains of the big days of coal mining, at its best in the 80's. The excitement was all over by 1900 and the place has settled quietly back since then.

Wilkeson is easily accessible and well worth a visit.

OLD GREEK CHURCH
with double cross still is
sometimes used for
services.

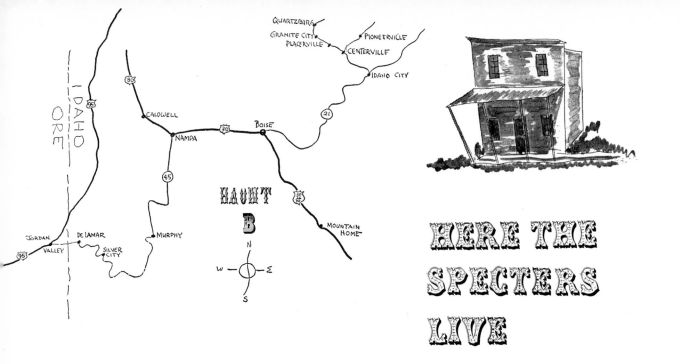

HERE THE
SPECTERS
LIVE

SILVER CITY, IDAHO

Here is a dead town still having enough buildings to line the streets and give a semblance of its former robust self. Some are big—the Idaho Hotel, the school and many others. All are weathered and all have the picturesque look of a ghost town. Its history is turbulent, full of shootings between rival mining companies and strife between men and management. As a result of these troubles and many epidemics, the cemeteries above Slaughter House Gulch are well populated and full of the typical wrought-iron enclosures of the day.

The main hotels, the Idaho and War Eagle, seem to have been "assembled" a room at a time with no original plan. The latter is about gone, except for its "Samson's War Eagle Annex" across the street.

The brewery just below the latter could find no room for its storage vats on the same side of the street, so they were built on the other side, underground, and a pipe line carried the beverage under the street.

One of the largest livery stables is on the bank of Jordan Creek; horses were taken to water over a pathway still visible.

The same stream runs right under the middle of the large Masonic Hall, and it was a favorite joke to go in the back door, come out the front. Then one had "crossed over the Jordan."

Some of the mine yields were almost unbelievable. The Poorman mine alone produced ore, assaying $5,000 a ton, so easily turned it could be cut like lead. Until 1875 its production was more than $4,000,000. At that time the secretary decamped with funds and the records were stopped until 1888 when the mine reopened with a new secretary.

Even in 1889, with its main glory dimming, Silver City still had six general stores, a tin shop, two meat markets, the two hotels, four restaurants, a photographers' gallery, the brewery, a bottling plant, a jeweler, the *Owyhee Avalanche* newspaper, two lumber yards, a tailor shop, three barbershops, four lawyers, two doctors and eight saloons. Also there was a section not mentioned in the boasting paragraphs of the newspaper. This was an exceptionally large "Virgin's Alley." Some of the houses in this section were luxurious; more plush than many of the residences. Most of the girls were segregated, but some had little "cribs" of their own on the hill. At least one married

EVEN "PLAZA" IN CENTER of town has old mine shaft in center. Tailings dumps of one of larger mines shows on opposite hill. Rockhounds love to comb dumps; sources have provided items like 15-pound crystal of pyragyrite sent to Paris exposition in 1866. Gem was found in Poorman mine.

man discovered here was added to the population above Slaughter House Gulch by his wife.

Silver City lost its position as county seat in 1935. This was a final crushing blow to a city already flat on its back and the place entered the ranks of the Ghosts.

On the way in after an almost endless series of switchbacks on a narrow dirt road, a splendid view of the city may be had from War Eagle Mountain. Silver City certainly ranks with Elkhorn, Montana; Bodie, California and St. Elmo, Colorado in size and interest.

"SILVER SLIPPER" SALOON to left, drugstore, center, courthouse and jail right.   Final shut-down was in 1942.

OLD CHURCH HAS BEEN Protestant and Catholic at various times.

WINTERS WERE RUGGED in Silver City and snows deep. Trip to "little house in back" was rendered easier by covered connection to residence.

SILVER CITY, IDAHO. Building at left is newspaper office of *Owyhee Avalanche.* At right is Masonic Hall. First lodge was formed Oct., 1865. Town flourished for about 70 years, beginning about 1860. Now only constable lives there. $4,000,000 in silver was produced by 1875.

FIRE PROTECTION was of simplest in "Idaho Hotel."

OLD SCHOOL IS ONE of best preserved of many buildings in Silver City.

STORE IN SILVER CITY, IDAHO. Effect of carving has been achieved by tacking odd-shaped pieces of wood to false front. Building is unique in its ornamentation.

IDAHO CITY, IDAHO

The Boise basin area in and around Idaho City produced more gold during its good years than all of Alaska, according to local authority, the total being some $100,000,000. The population of Idaho City during its boom years (1865 to 1888) was 4,800. The town was proud to claim Idaho's first Masonic hall, first newspaper buildings, first Catholic church and that extremely necessary item for gold rush towns a jail, also Idaho's first!

There were several elegant theaters with private boxes furnished with chairs having plush seats. The 23 law offices were kept busy with the constant litigation over claims and location boundaries common to boom towns. Four breweries and 41 saloons kept the dust down in the throats of the miners and six livery stables rented hacks and surreys for elegant Sunday trips around the limited roads in the area. The best known of all the buildings of the era is gone, having been built of logs, subject to decay. This was the Territorial jail. It stood in an enclosed acre of ground. Besides the main "cellblock" there were utility sheds, cook-house, storage and a large cemetery. This last handily received the victims of fast-moving justice and hangings, all of which were carried out on the premises. "Road agents," highwaymen who held up and plundered the stages between the several towns in the Boise Basin, were so bad that for a time even Wells Fargo had to suspend operations. Noteworthy was "Teddy White," a terror to passengers and freight haulers. Idaho City's history bears a strong resemblance to that of Bannack, Montana. It is a coincidence that Idaho City started out under the name of Bannock City!

Several bad fires have removed many

LARGE PINE TREES which have grown up inside grave enclosures attest to distant date of burial.

LIGHTING REVEALS many details of beautiful wrought-iron gate in old Idaho City cemetery.

of the hotels and theaters of early day as well as many other wooden structures. The worst one was called the "Great Fire." Sweeping through the town, the holocaust seemed as though it would destroy the city completely. One of the buildings b u r n e d was the first post office. This had been on Main street. It was rebuilt a block away from there the same y e a r by Postmaster Jas Pinney. Brick used was burned in a kiln on Elk Creek. Most of the brick buildings still standing today owe their origin to these same ovens.

The road from Boise is good, particularly interesting are the old dredge dumps noticeable on Moore's Creek, which rushes alongside the highway.

DREDGE TAILINGS REFLECTED in Moore's Creek show typical structure, clearly delineated by early morning side-lighting.

FIRST CATHOLIC CHURCH in Idaho stands in direct sun against threatening sky.

PLACERVILLE, IDAHO

Mr. Robinson started a store in Placerville in 1874, during the time of Placerville's growing pains and greatest prosperity. Still operating today, the store is run by his grandaughter, Mrs. Henrietta Penrod, who is also postmistress.

Instead of the usual main street, this town had an open square or plaza, such as you might see in Mexico. But instead of adobe brick, these establishments were built of logs and whip-sawed lumber and mostly had false fronts. Several on the north side were built of stone and are in a good state of preservation. Of the original three saloons, the Magnolia still stands.

In early days, it is related, a weary traveler, probably a prospector, came in to Placerville with his string of animals. Seeing the well at the corner of the long porch fronting the Magnolia, he stopped, grateful for the chance to drink. The usual group of idlers sat and stood on the porch watching. One of these, a rowdy who had imbibed more than his share of the beverages served inside, decided to make sport of the stranger, thus showing off to his cronies. Before the thirsty man from the hills could reach the bucket, the rowdy grabbed it and threw the contents in the stranger's face. While the group roared, the wet and dazed man reached for his gun, but was shot dead by the tough before he could see to aim.

There was a trial of sorts, the verdict "Innocent by reason of self-defense." It would have been a lot of trouble to haul the culprit miles to the nearest jail in Idaho City. Besides it was all in a spirit of good, clean fun.

Placerville had 29 places where liquor could be bought in those days, besides the three saloons and three hotels. Currency wasn't always available and a lot of everyday business transactions were done in gold dust by the 3,000 people who once lived here.

METAL ROOF HAS PRE-SERVED Magnolia saloon from fate suffered by many other buildings in Placerville, that of rotting to ground.

PIONEERVILLE, IDAHO

Accurately named, Pioneerville was the original settlement of any consequence in the famously rich Boise Basin.

The first band of hardy prospectors and miners were so carried away in their excitement over the amounts of gold panned out in the stream-bed, that they didn't lay in supplies enough to get through the winter when deep snows would isolate them.

A stockade of sorts was rudely and hastily thrown together and a delegation sent to the nearest source of supplies. The remaining men hardly dared venture out of the shelter so harrassed were they by hostile Indians.

When the supplies at last arrived, the first cases opened were those containing that heartening staple, whiskey.

The leader of the whole enterprise was J. Marion Moore. His name is still attached to the stream which flows past Idaho City. In fact, the latter was originally called Moore's Creek, then Moorestown.

Ores in Pioneer City, by now Pioneerville, assayed $20,000 to the ton for the richest samples. This was when the town was touted as the busiest camp in Boise Basin.

But somehow the lodes seemed to come quickly to an end and Placerville drew away much of the population, being larger by this time and boasting more and fancier "emporiums" as well as beautiful girls who could be pinched for a pinch of "dust" or a nugget.

Pioneerville shrivelled, though getting a "shot-in-the-arm" later by the introduction of dredges in the streams. These plowed the deeper deposits of gold in the gravels and left the usual desolation. Even now you will pass a huge dredge standing idle in the stream, as you wend your dusty way to Pioneerville.

DREDGE, LONG IDLE, squats in tiny pool of stream below Pioneerville. Miles of dumps downstream attest industrious digestion of gold-bearing gravels.

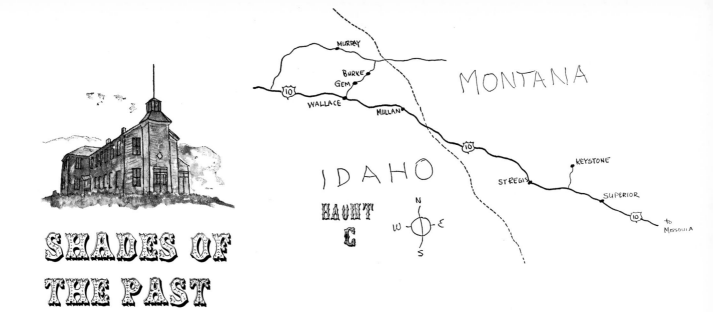

GEM AND BURKE, IDAHO

Gem shares with its neighbor up Canyon Creek, Burke, a situation so narrow that it is nearly all length and little width.   The street, railroad and creek occupy almost the entire space between crowding canyon walls.

Old buildings, some dating from the town's inception in 1886, were squeezed into available spots between the road and cliff.

In the busy and violent days of Gem, each of the larger buildings (and many more since vanished) contained a saloon.

The period before the turn of century was filled with strife between the mines' management and labor.   Gem then had a population of 2,500.

The remains of mining and milling machinery stand forlornly rusting on the banks of the stream.

Many old mining towns are strung out in a narrow line, squeezed into the confines of a cramped space along the stream where gold was originally found as "color" in some prospector's pan.

Burke is an example of this sort of construction.   In the days when the railroad ran many busy passenger coaches the length of the town, it was said the store owners used to have to hurry out and roll up their awnings before the train could pass by.

Certainly, when the big hotel was built it was forced to straddle the tracks, the trains then running right through the middle of it! The hotel is now gone with the heyday of Burke, as are many of the old buildings. Not that there is any lack of picturesque old false fronts, but one must search them out.   The railroad station itself is a gem, with its classic nineteenth century waiting room now full of house plants instead of people.

BRIDGE CROSSED STREAM thick with tailings from Hecla Mine above. Red-brick structure faces other way on only, narrow street. It was first post office in Gem, then grocery. Later it served for years as warehouse for Hecla Mine.

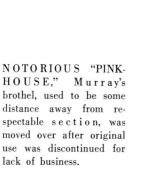

NOTORIOUS "PINK-HOUSE," Murray's brothel, used to be some distance away from respectable section, was moved over after original use was discontinued for lack of business.

MURRAY, IDAHO

It is almost unbelievable how fast a town can burgeon after a big strike of gold. Murray was a good example of this kind of mushroom growth. In 1883 color showed up in a wandering prospector's gold pan which had been dipped in Prichard Creek. There wasn't another soul around on that day, unless you count the prospector's burro! But within two years 2,000 people called the place home.

Flimsy tents were first dwellings and stores, to be intermingled with log cabins with sod roofs; then a sawmill produced whip-sawed lumber from plentiful timber around the site and false-fronts appeared. This motley main street was filled with life, miners, some wives and children, many "fancy women," horses, mules and wagons all competing for space. Then wooden walks were built, separating human and animal traffic. Clouds of dust rose in summer, in fall and spring the wagons sank hub deep in mud and winters saw the snow pile up several feet deep in drifts.

While all this was going on, the stream was being ravaged to its very bedrock bones by dredges and placer hoses. The returns were huge. Gold seemed to fill the spaces between river cobblestones. Then came the inevitable and these rich deposits came to an end in that same decade. Murray, in this short interval since its inception, had become the County Seat but the honor was short lived. With the depletion of gold in Prichard Creek, people quickly moved on to more fertile fields and the seat of county government was lost in 1898. Gaps appeared between buildings where structures burned or were razed. In a last-ditch effort to present a brave front, Murray moved its now scattered structures together, closing ranks in a futile and pitiful struggle to postpone the inevitable end. Depletion continued, however, and not many structures remain now.

THE MURRAY FIRE DEPARTMENT had two of these then modern rigs in the 80's. Murray fire laddies took their hose carts to Spokane, Wash., for drill exhibitions, won prize two years in row. Little bell on top tinkles as cart is wheeled over bumps.

POTOSI GULCH, IDAHO

Most of the earliest gold discoveries were made in the bottom of a pan which had scooped up some wet gravel from a tiny stream in some "gulch." To the early day prospectors every canyon or small valley was a "gulch" and many a town sprang into life on the spot where "color" showed in the pan. Potosi Gulch was one of these. It quickly burgeoned and almost as quickly it wilted and died. But while it lived, Potosi was a rendezvous for all the usual camp hangers-on. It had a large boardinghouse, a saloon and several business establishments.

Now only a log cabin remains below the tiny cemetery on the point overlooking the once roistering camp. Since there are only two graves, perhaps those early disputes in old Potosi fizzled out before gun play developed.

WHEN THIS CABIN is gone, so will be Potosi Gulch.

KEYSTONE, MONTANA

Keystone was first called Carter, when the rich silver lode was discovered in the 80's and was quite a place, "wild as they come," about 1900. But peace certainly reigns there now.

The few remaining buildings are very scattered, but the location of the main street could be figured out by the store and a cabin or two on the other side. Some larger houses, beautifully weathered, stand leaning at various angles here and there. A large barn, partly flattened, is surrounded by nettles and brambles.

KEYSTONE GENERAL Merchandise Emporium marks site of Main Street.

GARNET, MONTANA

Garnet has been resurrected from seemingly permanent ghostliness at least twice. As of this writing it holds a place among the top Ghost Towns of the West, but it could be revived again.

Population: two people and two eager, friendly dogs. The human residents of Garnet are Mr. and Mrs. Clifford Dahl who, with the first flake of snow, move down to Drummond, leaving the town completely to its memories. "The snow comes down like white corn flakes and in no time is ten feet deep."

An imposing three-story hotel lords it over the saloons, stores and other business houses. The warm red coloring of long-weathered wood seems especially pronounced here. Some of the structures lean one way, some another, some seem in imminent danger of collapse, and indeed several have collapsed.

But, it is fairly easy to repopulate the town and imagine the surreys again rolling up and down the steep streets.

Garnet's wealth was in gold and they took millions out in the years following the original discoveries in 1862. There would have been even more, but so many of the men were too drunk to work much of the time. The mine that turned out the richest, the "Nancy Hanks," was owned by two partners, one of whom was much addicted to alcohol. After one protracted spree the other partner bought him out for $50. In the several years following, the "Nancy Hanks" spewed out $10,000,000 in gold. The retired partner had moved down to Beartown, and one day when another load of rich ore from the mine rolled past his door he hanged himself.

F. A. Davy operated the Garnet General Store for 45 years. He was not popular with the children of the town. They hanged him in effigy from the flagpole of the hotel,

HALL OF HOTEL was entrance to three-story building. Door stands open to weather.

and you can still see some ragged remains of the stingy merchant's proxy hanging there. Mr. Davy also ran the Garnet Stage Line and Garnet Freight Line. He died here years ago. About 1912 a large part of town burned down and never was rebuilt. The "Nancy Hanks" operated off and on, closing entirely in 1954.

The flavor of the town itself is not reminiscent of anything like such a late era. The buildings all date from earlier days.

It was in those times that the combined population from Coloma (above Garnet) down to Beartown was nearly five thousand people. And it was during one of those hard winters the snow came down so hard and so long that supplies ran out. When things began to get really desperate, one brave individual put on his miner's light, went down into the maze of shafts and tunnels, and made his way through one connection after another until he had gone the whole eleven miles to Beartown and arranged for supplies to be sent up. A deed on that high order would seem to make up a little for some of the wildness that was Garnet.

The sharp switchbacks and steep approach to Garnet are called the "Chinee" Grade. The story is that a Chinese miner stached a sizable fortune there, concealed in a five-pound baking powder can. It has never been found.

LEFT IS KELLY'S SALOON, r i g h t barber shop and drugstore combination.

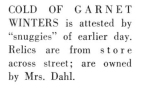

COLD OF G A R N E T WINTERS is attested by "snuggies" of earlier day. Relics are from s t o r e across street; are owned by Mrs. Dahl.

BEARTOWN, MONTANA

Here is a town almost vanished from the sight of man, yet the phrase "as bad as a Beartown Tough" remains potent to the ears of Montanans. The gang known by that name terrorized the citizens not only of their own town, but also of Garnet, at the upper end of the canyon, and Bearmouth at the bottom. They were never really subdued, making trouble over a long period of time.

The canyon is narrow, hardly offering room for more than the gravel road, but at one point not far below the notorious "Chinee Grade," a side stream enters. Here is somewhat more level ground, and here was laid out the collection of stores, saloons, hotels and brothels that was Beartown. The wonder is that the ground suppported the town, so honeycombed it was by mine tunnels. These extended the entire length of the canyon.

The site of the mill is now indicated by scanty foundations and a pile of boards, the center of town can be traced by a board here and there and basements nearly filled with rubble and brush. Across the stream is the only structure anywhere near intact, the jail, formerly a powder house.

Odd that this token of Beartown badmen should survive along with bloody memory of those "Beartown Toughs," who have been so long under the sod that their very headboards have melted away.

THE BEARTOWN JAIL

BEARMOUTH, MONTANA

A town dependent upon one industry or source of income is deserted when that source fails. Further, a town serving another depends upon the continuance of its supporter.

So, when Garnet died, Bearmouth also faded away. The fabulously rich ores in Garnet all through the 60's, 70's and 80's poured down the "Chinee Grade" to Bearmouth, to be shipped to smelters.

Garnet had its ups and downs in common with other mining camps, and with each demise and each resurgence, Bearmouth followed suit. It did have one steady business, as a main stop for stagecoaches on the old Mullan Road. This meant an Inn, a beautiful two-story, balconied structure, and at least one large livery stable. In addition to lodgings for man and beast, a blacksmith shop was called for.

The hostelry and livery stable still stand, conveniently near each other.

Time was when the open spaces surrounding these buildings were filled solidly with pleasure houses of various types, all rowdy. It was a treat for the hard-working miners "up on the mountain" in Garnet or Beartown to come down for a weekend spree in "Bear's Mouth," as it was first called.

OLD STAGECOACH STOP and inn. Building is tenanted and in good repair. TV antenna adds modern touch.

THEY BUILT SOLIDLY in old days. Detail of corner of livery stable.

LATE AFTERNOON SUN leaves fronts of old Rimini buildings in shadow. Famous for gold, much silver and lead has also come from mountain towering above town.

RIMINI, MONTANA

The gravel road leading to Rimini from the highway is amazingly level, of the easiest grades and curves. The mystery of this unusual approach to a mountain town is explained by the two Scott brothers who have lived there since 1896. The Northern Pacific had a railroad in Rimini already when Jim Hill got the idea he would run his line in too. He had already graded the whole right of way when he ran into so much trouble with the other line he gave up.

The townspeople built a dam above the town to have a water supply and one night the dam broke. A wall of water came rushing down the canyon. There was only one cabin in its path and it was demolished. Fortunately, the owner was suffering from dysentery and had gone to the backhouse on the side of the hill and so his life was spared.

Rimini now is a true Ghost Town along its main street fronted by a line of false-fronted buildings, all abandoned. There are a few houses on the next street to the west, some of which have the usual quota of summer residents. A very few, including the Scott brothers, are permanent.

MARYSVILLE, MONTANA

Here is a town, now almost completely a ghost, which in the 80's and 90's was Montana's leading gold producer and teemed with 3,000 people. It had several streets with one centering a substantial business district, with stone and brick buildings housing the bank, Masonic Hall, drugstore, hotels and the inevitable saloons. At the south end were several imposing frame structures, false fronted, one of which held a large newspaper plant. The remaining two of this group are most picturesque, weathered and worn, but still standing upright, albeit at opposite angles. In front of them is something unique in mining camps, an athletic field with rickety bleachers still standing! Not all of the hard-working, early-day miners spent all their spare time in saloons and brothels. There were bearded western baseball players and bearded western baseball fans too!

The Methodist and Catholic churches stand almost side by side across from the school.

The brick and stone buildings mentioned before line a block on one side and are in fairly good shape, but none does any business. The second floor of the saloon boasts rather large windows, one of which shows an old pool table, long idle.

At one side of the town stands the imposing mill of the old Drumlummon Mine. Its history is the history of the town, although there were others. Thomas Cruse in 1876 discovered the ledge and named it for his native town in Ireland and the town for Mary Ralston, the first woman in the place. Total production from Drumlummon is estimated to have been about $50,000,000.

As usual, the few remaining inhabitants of Marysville still believe there are further rich bodies of gold close by, and chances are good that they are right. Until these are found, and gold advances in price, the town peacefully disintegrates.

IT HAS BEEN LONG SINCE exciting ball games were played on the brush grown diamond. Bleachers still stand.

LEFT TO RIGHT, WERE BANK, Masonic Hall with drugstore below, the post office, then the stone grocery store building. Little structure w i t h balcony served as doctor's office.

METHODIST CHURCH, left, and Catholic edifice, right, stand companionably close.

CLANCEY, MONTANA

A modern term, the "metropolitan area" is aptly used to describe the collection of tiny old towns, and the more imposing hub that was Clancey. Clancey *was* comparatively important in the nineties, which were *very* gay, at least in the confines of several bordellos.

Communities fringing Clancey did not have many substantial buildings, for their people went to Clancey, which served as a "shopping center" and "recreational area." Consequently, when these satellites died, their very bones crumbled to dust and some are hard to find. "Lump City," for example, is only a small group of holes in the ground where houses once stood. Alhambra has fared only slightly better, with its one remaining building.

But Clancey, being on the highway, still breathes. It has a filling station, a tiny garage, a couple of stores, and the little church.

In Clancey's robust days, the Liverpool Mine was the dominating factor in the economy of the whole area, although many lesser mines and dumps scarred the countryside. During its period of prosperity the Liverpool produced $1,500,000 in silver, and it was done the hard way. The ore was hauled by bull team to Fort Benton, thence by river and ocean to Swansea, Wales, to be refined in the world-famed smelters there. The raw stuff was rich enough to pay a profit after all that!

LITTLE CHURCH in Clancey still serves tiny congregation.

ALHAMBRA STORE once served wide area, had everything from kerosene lamps to bed "comforters." Town is one of small satellites orbiting around Clancey.

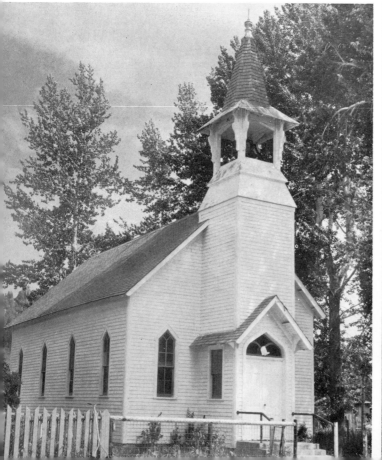

LEFT IS THE livery stable and right the meat market.

WICKES, MONTANA

Here is a town that has had more than its share of disastrous fires having been all but wiped out in the holocaust years of 1901, 1906, and 1910.

The town is picturesque enough in its little group of remaining buildings, but its main interest lies in the ruins of the huge smelters and refineries, the domed coke ovens and piles of cannonball-like grinder used in the ore-pulverizing process.

These operations turned out $50,000,000 in silver and gold. The nearby Alta Mine produced $32,000,000 in silver and gold. The Gregory, with a record of $9,000,000, is in the neighborhood, as are the Nina and Bertha. The early 1890's saw the end of almost all operations.

ELKHORN, MONTANA

Here is a real, honest-to-goodness Ghost Town. The main street winds steeply up a rocky slope, to end abruptly at the bottom of huge tailing dumps below the big mine and mill. Beyond that rises even steeper the shoulder of Elkhorn Mountain, covered on its slope with blue spruce, pine and aspen. At the summit the bare rocks above timberline would be early under snow and covered into summer.

On both sides of the street straggle lines of old and weathered buildings. The roofs of some are caved in, the windows mostly without glass, and doors missing or hanging by one hinge.

Several are two stories tall and attics add to their height, giving them a gaunt, cadaverous look. Inside, long strips of imported, once elegant wallpaper hang in tatters to flap dismally in the unhindered wind.

Elkhorn has been dead for sixty years except for desultory flare-ups of activity, and it is hard to picture the frenzy that gripped the area in 1870 when yellow flakes of gold were discovered in the creek running beside the town.

Panning in the stream soon changed to hard rock mining when the quartz lodes were discovered, and the building of the town, its stores, 14 saloons, several churches and lodge halls proceeded at a furious pace.

Transportation was next to impossible and only the barest necessities came in for a long time, but in 1889 the Northern Pacific drove a line up to the 5,500-foot high city, running in three trains a week.

During these productive years, the flow of mineral wealth in gold and silver totaled some $14,000,000.

FALSE-FRONTED "emporium" stands in sagging ruin along Main Street.

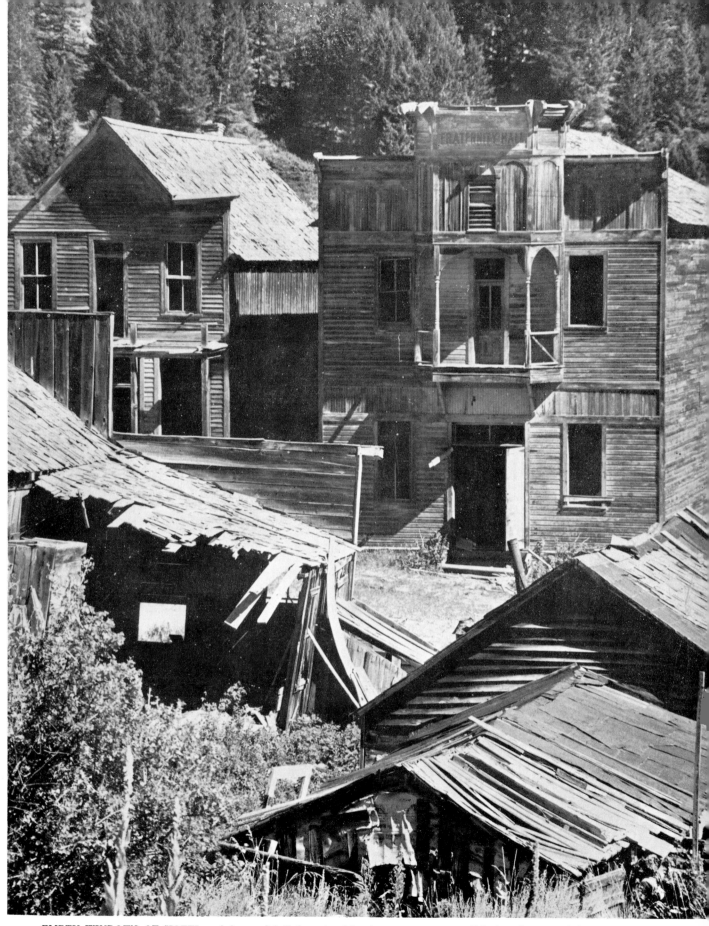

EMPTY WINDOWS OF HOTEL and fraternal hall face tiny false fronts across street. Telephoto lens aimed from hill back of town brings buildings into perspective.

MILL BUILDINGS of big-producing Elkhorn Mine, seen from assay office. Only ghosts now rest in chair on porch.

GRANITE, MONTANA

Philipsburg is much too alive to qualify as a "dead" Ghost Town. But it is contemporary with one of the most interesting of Montana's historic camps, Granite, and figures so much in its history that it cannot be ignored.

About 16 miles southwest are the sapphire deposits of the Rock Creek area. These gems are found in gravels of several "Gulches," Anaconda, Sapphire and others. When the stones were first discovered about 1892 the usual exaggerated, excited announcements were made as to size, "rich deep color," etc. The stones actually run rather small, ranging from ¼ to ½ inch, with a sprinkling of larger ones.

The gems were first discovered in routine placering operations for gold, and are still being obtained by variations of hydraulic and sluicing operations.

From 1899 to 1900, 400,000 carats were recovered from the sluiceboxes. Of this amount about 25,000 carats were suitable for faceting, the remainder being put to commercial use, as for watch jewels. For this latter use, the Montana sapphires were in demand as they required less work to ready them and brought $2.00 to $6.00 per ounce.

The bank of Granite has vanished entirely, but the vault remains. Its heavy iron doors have become unhinged and the old records have blown all over the mountaintop site of the town. Among them are many billheads marked "Philipsburg Foundry" with the dates all through the 80's and 90's. Bowen and Thompson were the "Prop'rs" and listed such cryptic items as Battery Shoes, Spiders, R. B. Keys and 5-foot Strate Bars. These items and hundreds more were billed every few days to the Granite Mountain Mining Co., and the concern must have provided the lifeblood for the upkeep of the mines of Old Granite.

Situated almost on the very top of a mountain, Granite affords a splendid view.

Mr. Henry Kistle has lived in this mountaintop aerie since his arrival there in 1899, at the age of nine. He was born in the old camp, Elkhorn. He says that the town hit its peak in 1892, with 3,600 people. "It turned out $60,000,000 in silver," he said, "though other sources do not agree with this. Some people say only $58,000,000."

There was lots of money around, anyway. A Mr. Fisher kept a herd of cows down in the valley and made trips up here every day with milk. This, being a real luxury, brought a good price, and at the end

MINER'S UNION HALL gets early sunshine on mountaintop situation. Stairway to upper floor leads from door at right. Rear of building is approaching ruin.

MINE ACCIDENTS WERE FREQUENT and required large hospital. "Little house" in front seems conspicuous, but there was no room for it in back.

of the month he would make his collections amounting to a lot of money. One time he had $480.00 and was held up by bandits on the way down. He wouldn't give up his money, so they shot him in the chest and took it. But he lived to tell the story.

VAULT IS ALL that remains of Bank of Granite.

SUBSTANTIAL STONE HOUSE was headquarters of Granite Mines superintendent. Street was "Silk Stocking Lane" with line of cribs for girls.

EXTENSIVE STONE FOUNDATIONS fill site of Granite. Wooden remains here identify building as church.

TRAMWAY AND TAILINGS dumps of old bi-metallic mine are still in evidence, sometimes still yield beautiful specimens of granite heavily laced with pure silver. Left foreground is livery stable with buggies still inside.

PHILIPSBURG, MONTANA

ALMOST ALL THE BUILDINGS of the town are of that early vintage and many are v a c a n t. T h e r e is enough atmosphere to merit a visit, particularly since it is the take-off site for Granite.

PHILIPSBURG RETAINS much atmosphere of the old mining camp days.

THE LAND OF GOLDEN GHOSTS

SOUTHERN CROSS, MONTANA

High on the shoulder of Iron Mountain is the ghostly gold camp called Southern Cross. The name is unique among the old mining towns; surely some sailor, back from sea, must have bestowed the starry title.

It was lively enough in the days when Tillie Riemenschnieder and her husband, Albert, lived nearby. Tillie lives quietly now in Portland, Ore., but remembers vividly those booming times when gold was pouring out of the shafts and tunnels, and the big boardinghouse in the center of town was the scene of wild revelry on Saturday nights.

Tillie lived five miles up the canyon formed between Cable and Rumsey mountains. She and Albert occupied a comfortable five-room log house, and if enough cases of food had been stored, they spent the winters in near isolation there. If supplies ran low, Albert donned his six-foot snowshoes and went down to Southern Cross for more.

The train from Anaconda came only halfway in winter and then just once a week. At the end of the line it was met by a large horse-drawn sleigh. This had a covered cab equipped with a little stove. The passengers huddled around this tiny warmth in heavy fur coats, trying to be comfortable in temperatures often 30 degrees below. Winter lasted from October to June, with very heavy snowfalls.

Now the town is reduced to the boardinghouse, the mill and a block of "main street." A large fallen pine blocks the door to the old Post Office, but no one looks for mail, anyway.

STAIRS LEADING NO-WHERE and little false front are part of remains of "Southern Cross."

REMAINING BUILDINGS in Mammoth are of log construction. Central one is saloon, others stores, livery stable at end of street.

MAMMOTH, MONTANA

Mammoth's one street is lined with a number of old false-front stores, the post office, saloon and blacksmith shop. Several log cabins are strung along above, below and on the other side. Some of these latter are kept in repair and a little colony of refugees from hotter areas spend their vacations here in the shadow of the several snowy peaks which tower above the town.

The store buildings remain strictly untouched, and except for weathering, must look much as they did at the turn of the century. At that time the mines were turning out more than 14,000,000 dollars in gold and silver, mostly produced by the Mammoth. This was located on the very steep mountainside above the town, and plainly visible still are the remains of the tramway which carried on a continuously busy procession of cars up and down.

Mammoth somehow missed out on the temporary revival which came to many camps in the 30's and has remained almost unchanged all these years.

MELROSE, MONTANA

Melrose likely would have died entirely long before now, but being on a main highway, many of the old log houses and cabins are still occupied. A store or two and a filling station make up the business center.

The town was not a mining camp itself, but served several big ones as a supply center. Notable among these is Hecla.

Melrose is placed at an elevation of 5,173 feet, and this, with its position in this part of the Rockies some twenty miles from the Continental Divide makes for a heavy snowfall in the winter. The original buildings after the usual tent and shack stage were of logs. They are typical of this part of Montana, and have survived many severe winters. The chinking was done with a snow-white mortar and this, alternated with the dark logs, makes for a striking striped effect.

The Big Hole River, which runs close by, is famed for Rainbow trout and locations requiring some leg work still yield good catches.

In the early days, any conspicuous valley carved out of the mountains was dubbed a "Hole." Melrose is in one of these, larger than most. And, therefore, the name for the area and the river became the Big Hole.

PIONEER LOG AND SOD HOUSE surmounted by television aerial produces ludicrous anachronism. Note also hospitable touch, light fixture at door. Structure is one of earliest homes in Melrose.

VIRGINIA CITY, MONTANA

The date was May 26, the year 1863. It was about four o'clock in the afternoon. Bill Fairweather had been "elected" the leader of the group of six miners searching for gold. Bill was young, husky and had "a good personality." He had no trouble giving orders, and now he gave one that made history. "There's a piece of bedrock projecting and we had better go over and see if we can't get enough money to buy a little tobacco." He dug enough dirt to fill a pan, sending Henry Edgar to the stream to wash it out. The spade work done, he poked around some more with a butcher knife and found color enough to make him shout, *"I've found a scad!"*

Henry's pan was only half empty but it was already obvious that he, also, had a bonanza. The group feverishly finished washing it and two others before it got dark. The three pans of gravel produced twelve dollars worth of gold.

VIRGINIA CITY HAS plenty of atmosphere provided by original buildings.

Next day the six panned out $180 and on the next staked out their claim. Then they went to Bannack for supplies. The prospectors fully intended to keep their discovery a deep secret, but the find must have been written all over their faces. Everyone was their bosom friend! They, followed by a cavalcade, started back to the diggin's June 2 and arrived June 6. They named the place "Alder Creek" because of a group of those trees on the bank of the gulch.

The village which sprang up in true early-day, boom-town style was first called "Varina" and then, legally "Virginia."

When millions in gold began to pour out of the gulch, the only road to ship it over was the one to Bannack, infested by Plummer's gang of brigands. It was the robbery and killing of Nicholas Thiebalt for $200 that lit the fuse under the seething townsmen. For this crime, George Ives was strung up. His neck was replaced in the noose by that of another and another until most of the outlaws at the Virginia end were disposed of. Others were hung at Laurin and Bannack, the latter seeing the end of Plummer himself.

The Vigilantes had done a good job, but were "carried away" by their successes and later went too far with their summary carrying out of "Justice" and fell into disrepute.

After this, Virginia led a more peaceful existence with only a few killings, these mostly having been committed in the heat of anger or in self-defense and therefore "excusable."

The town never died entirely, and now likely never will, it having become a tourist attraction.

WHILE THE BUILDING WAS yet unfinished, part of Plummer's notorious crew was hanged from exposed beam.

THIS COULD BE one of the stages harassed by Plummer gang on road between Virginia City and Bannack.

LAURIN, MONTANA

Laurin is one of the group of mining camps spawned by the rich strikes of the general area called Alder Gulch. These included the better-known Virginia City and Alder itself.

Old tailings almost the whole length of the gulch attest to the persistent workings of the equipment once operated by Harvard University, so richly rewarded in the several millions in gold extracted from the stream bed.

The original gold discoveries were in May 1863, and the gulch p r o d u c e d $10,000,000 during the first year.

Laurin shared in this bonanza and for a time was the El Dorado of the entire area, but it has now dwindled greatly and the old relics are hard to find among buildings of a somewhat more modern vintage.

Two of the notorious Plummer gang of road agents were hanged here, on July 4, 1864. These two were "Red" Yager and G. W. Brown.

Everywhere you go in the area around Virginia City you seem to find places where members of the unholy terrorists were hanged. This is because frontier outlaws were frequently hanged almost on the spot where apprehended.

LAURIN HAS SOME modern buildings but here and there can be found some dating to turbulent early days. Rain makes flat, grey light on old false front.

AT THE RIGHT OF brick hotel is Skinner's Saloon, once hangout of notorious Plummer gang. At right stood building housing first territorial legislature of Montana, now gone.

BANNACK, MONTANA

In addition to being the first capital, Bannack claims several other firsts. Back from the street in discreet seclusion is the first jail, a really primitive one-story, sod-roofed structure. The little false-fronted Skinner's Saloon served both its advertised purpose and as headquarters for Henry Plummer and his outlaw gang. Plummer's masquerade as head of all useful and law-abiding citizens is one of the most incredible episodes in the history of the west.

The stretch of road between Bannack and Virginia City was the scene of more holdups, robberies and murders than almost any other comparable stagecoach route. The outlaw gang made up of ruffians with prices on their heads were strung along the route and relayed information to one another, so that no coach stood a chance of getting through.

This murderous crew had for its mastermind the Sheriff of Bannack! Henry Plummer was also an escapee, having fled from the camps of California and Nevada. In Bannack he started life anew. To the populace he set himself up as a preserver of the peace, guardian of law and order. He soon became official sheriff, built the jail and had rings put in the floor so that prisoners could not escape merely by punching a hole in the sod-roof. His home became a symbol of hospitality, the scene of receptions and dances for the "upper crust" of Bannack. Even the Governor of the Territory of Montana was entertained there.

At the same time, behind this screen of respectability, Plummer pulled the strings that ended in over a hundred murders and a bonanza of money and jewelry taken from unfortunate stagecoach travelers.

At last, a roused committee of citizens formed the Vigilantes which unmasked Plummer and threw him into his own jail. His tenure therein was short. In short order a gallows was erected back of the saloon-rendezvous and the erstwhile sheriff was strung up. So were several of his henchmen, and they remain in close company under wooden headboards close by the gallows.

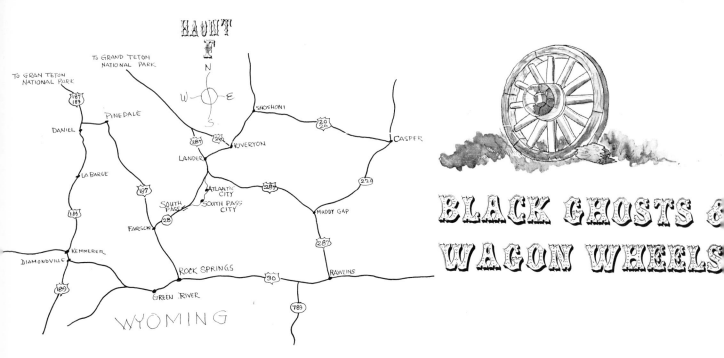

BLACK GHOSTS & WAGON WHEELS

DIAMONDVILLE, WYOMING

Gold and silver had no part in the early history of Diamondville; coal was what they dug a little to the north of town. No doubt Harrison Church was looking for gold when he dug into a good vein of coal in 1875 or thereabout. He alerted his backers in the east and they bought up the area. Though a boom seemed imminent, nothing much happened for twenty years when coal mining began in earnest.

Diamondville came into existence then, and at the turn of the century was as wild and boisterous as any gold camp. Its life spanned some forty years, but since the petering out of the vein, the city has faded away.

BRILLIANT, WELL-GROWN geraniums in pots and pans brighten windows of occupied old building.

NO FANCY "GINGER BREAD" adorns front of old saloon, and no frills were added to plain glass of whiskey. Plenty of trouble erupted from within in days when coal miners drew good pay, spent it on girls and liquor.

DIAMONDVILLE FIRE DEPARTMENT was on volunteer basis, had many calls to answer in bustling days. Often frame buildings, tinder dry, vanished in moments despite heroic efforts of tiny crew and inadequate equipment. Weeds grow undisturbed, now, in front of door.

ROCKING CHAIRS OF LODGERS used to creak on balcony of a summer evening, during tranquil periods of Diamondville's history. In times of trouble, labor strife and union disputes balcony served as safe vantage point.

SOUTH PASS CITY, WYOMING

The clear and rushing creek called Sweetwater figured prominently in early mining days. Gold had been found as early as 1842. Here the early pioneer-prospectors panned, while Indians watched from the rocks above. As they gathered their yellow flakes together and started East to "organize an outfit that would really develop the Sweetwater," they were often ambushed and killed by the silent watchers.

The white man muddied up the Indian's drinking water with his placerings and killed his food supply. The Indians didn't like it.

Retaliation came swiftly and often, but when the savage Sioux, Arapaho or Cheyenne rode into the now good-sized town of South Pass City, they found no women or children to carry off. What they didn't know was that a lookout was kept on the hill at all times, and at the approach of Indians, the women and children were herded into a cell behind the wine cellar, built into the side of hill, east of the store.

An old gentleman who lives nearby says that an old falling-down building was once a millinery shop. "The ladies liked to have the latest Paris hats then just like they do now. Only in those days it took a lot longer to get the hats out here. But then they stayed in style a lot longer, too."

In 1870, South Pass City had a population of 4,000, and was the county seat of Carter County which took in nearly a third of the whole state of Wyoming. One of the local citizens, William H. Bright, introduced the first bill to give women full right to vote in the state. And, in 1870, the first woman Justice of the Peace held court in South Pass City. She was never able to get hold of the docket from her predecessor, so she set the t o n e for her entire tenure by just starting out with a "clean new docket." The town's two doctors were part-time miners.

In a few short years, though, the town was deserted and the county seat was moved to Green River.

SAWN LUMBER was scarce in South Pass City.

NOT DATING BACK QUITE to earliest days, truck in old dump still has archaic look.

SENTRY WAS OFTEN POSTED on hill above town, to warn of Indian raids which were frequent. Little false front at left was "Millinery Shop" in its good years.

MAIN STREET of South Pass City.

ATLANTIC CITY, WYOMING

Looking down into Atlantic City, it is hard at first to see how such a good-sized town could once have covered both sides of the gulch.

But if you descend to the site and look into some of the quite substantial buildings —the Union Hall, the church, the bank—you begin to see where the rest of the town fitted into the empty spaces.

In 1868 several miners on a "bus-man's vacation" from South Pass City found a rather spectacular amount of color in Atlantic Ledge. In two years two thousand miners and the usual contingent of harlots and gamblers had populated the hillsides.

In another ten years it was mostly over; a few mills and mines kept going, but the bubble had burst and the scavengers moved on.

Now there are still some prospectors around, and summer vacationers, enough to hold occasional services in the tiny church on the hill, a quiet end to those short but hectic years.

THERE IS A "BOARDWALK" in Atlantic City, Wyoming, also.

ATLANTIC CITY TODAY shows gaps where once buildings solidly lined busy streets.

CHURCH, STILL SOMETIMES used by summer campers, dominates quiet scene; livery stable is at left.

GROVES OF ASPEN surround Atlantic City, Wyoming.

HYDE'S HALL WAS
SCENE of celebrations,
funerals, miners' meetings.

WHERE LIVE THE SILVER SPIRITS

KOKOMO, COLORADO

At Kokomo's elevation, 10,618 feet, deep snows cover the ground between November and May. In 1878 access routes were only narrow trails cut out of the sides of cliffs overhanging roaring streams.

But nothing could assuage the fever for gold that set in with the beginning of 1879. Men came in swarms to improvise shelters of the rudest description. These were set on top of six or eight feet of snow. Since surface indications were absent or out of sight under the snow, shafts were sunk at random on the first unclaimed site the prospective miner could lay hands on. And often, these paid off.

SALOON BEARS TRACES of bright orange paint, with black trim. Bar and tables remain intact. Upstairs "private rooms" were reached by less conspicuous door at side. Narrow gauge railroad passed close by; remains are seen crossing stream just past telephone pole, lower right.

With the opening of summer, Kokomo already had a population of 1,500! Prices of lots compared favorably with the altitude. A city government was organized, a bank built. Then followed saloons, hotels, stores, and sawmills. And before long, a newspaper and smelters.

The Kokomo Giant mine on Gold Hill had actually been producing ore rich enough to ship for smelting before this operation could be produced on the spot. The average assay was 179½ ounces of silver and 17.6 per cent lead. Gold showed only a trace in most of these ores. In this period of mining history standard gold sold at $18.60 per ounce and silver from $1.10 to $1.25.

By the time Kokomo was established, the mine owners had a large advantage over those of 1864, when labor was "outrageously high." Then, a miner, even though "indifferent and lazy," earned as much as $4.00 a day. Now a "more reasonable" scale was estab-

TYPICAL EARLY-DAY construction. House in Kokomo shows combination of log and whipsaw boards. Outdoor "plumbing" is at one side. Roof was steep, to better shed enormous snows of Rocky Mountain winters.

lished with the going rate of $2.00 to $2.25. And other commodities went back on a saner basis, with flour back to $2.25 per 100 pounds, candles $6.25 per box and nails five cents a pound, inflation was ended.

New strikes kept the frenzy unabated. One man who volunteered to dig a grave for a dead friend struck "mineral" and went to file a claim before burying his deceased comrade elsewhere.

Some companies constructed roasting furnaces at the mines, since the neighboring forests afforded fuel for the cutting. A stone wall two and a half feet high enclosed a space ten by twenty feet. In this was placed a floor of pine logs covered with finely split dry wood. About forty-five tons of ore were piled thereon and the wood beneath fired. Combustion continued for two weeks. When the sulphur and other refractory substances were expelled, the ore was then ready for smelting.

MASONIC HALL STANDS alone, facing sun, was even more ornate in Victorian days. "Gingerbread" has largely fallen, though window trims remain among most beautiful examples of art.

HILL ABOVE KOKOMO is honeycombed with mine tunnels and shafts. Two-story school, gauntly tall, dominates town. Just below is rear of Masonic Hall. Still lower is stream where casual panning started all excitement.

This prodigal use of the surrounding forests soon resulted in their depletion and wood had to come from farther away.

In the year 1881, when Kokomo had reached its population peak of 10,000, a disastrous fire raced through the wooden frame buildings of the town. Only a few structures were left standing. Rebuilding was started immediately, and for a time it seemed that the Kokomo of old was off to a fresh start. Much ore was still being taken from the mines and shipped by rail. But somehow the heart seemed to have gone out of the place and several mines faltered in production, it never reached the level of prosperity it had enjoyed before the fire and began gently to fold up.

LEADVILLE, COLORADO

When the Colorado historian and champion of Leadville, Caroline Bancroft, heard of my intent to include the Cloud City in this book she was alarmed.

I quote her warning, a paragraph of a letter in her always charming style. "But let me warn you, Leadville has 5,000 population. It is not a ghost town and never has been one. The population will blow its top if you call it one."

I wouldn't dare! But I again call attention to our chosen definition of a ghost, "a shadowy semblance of its former self."

And even if the city does not fit this category, how could one write anything bearing on Colorado's fabulous mining history without touching on Leadville, certainly no place in the State is so redolent. Besides, the city is now welcoming tourists with open arms. These will not stay away because of ghosts of those wilder, earlier days.

And so, with some trepidation, we proceed.

"Hang on to the Matchless, it will make millions again!"   As the Silver King of Colorado lay dying in the 90's, he whispered those hopeful words to "Baby Doe," but his world had already crashed around him.   And so had the luxurious bejeweled dream faded for his still beautiful wife.

The story of Horace Tabor and of his first and second wives, the pathetic, angular Augusta and the voluptuous Baby Doe is inextricably woven with that of Leadville.

The early discoveries of gold in "California Gulch," which supported Tabor and the future Leadville so poorly, the pushing aside of the hated heavy sands and carbonate, the discovery that these contained the real bonanzas, lead and silver, the fantastic returns from the hard rock mining and smelting of these hitherto neglected metals, were the factors that made Tabor and Leadville. The later failure of the early lodes, along with panics and silver crashes broke them.

Tabor, in the early 60's, had listened to the Siren Song of another gold strike in the mountains and had dragged Augusta out of her sickbed in Denver, piled her and their ailing baby into their rickety wagon and set out for the "shining peaks."

LEADVILLE, "THE CLOUD CITY" AS SEEN FROM Fryer Hill, looks as it did to Baby Doe.   Fryer Hill was named for Geo. H. Fryer, who, on April 4th, 1878 found carbonates here and named his claim the "New Discovery." Tailings dumps may be seen extending into town.

The cold, the bitter wind, the wails of the sick baby and her own miseries were endured with not too many complaints by Augusta, until they arrived in South Park. She later said it was "gorgeously beautiful." The night here was so cold that a little burro strayed into camp and got so close to the fire that he burned his fetlocks. Augusta cared for him and made him her pet, weeping on his sympathetic shoulder in her wretchedness and longing for her home in Maine.

On their arrival at camp in California Gulch, a cabin was thrown together, the pitiful, scrawny oxen slaughtered, the bag of dried apples opened up and Augusta started taking in boarders. The hard years dragged on, and then suddenly, *Bonanza!*

Tabor's partners, taken on in exasperation to get rid of them and their pleas for a "grubstake," had stumbled onto what would be the famous "Little Pittsburg" Mine. In two months the mine was bringing in $20,000 a week. The hard days were over, and with them, the marriage of Augusta and Horace.

Tabor, now risen to the status of a millionaire many times over, and Lt. Governor of Colorado, had a girl friend in the person of the glamorous Elizabeth McCourt, and certainly had no need for such a "dowdy, straitlaced drudge" as Augusta.

She was shed, not without some compensation financially, and the more rounded "Baby Doe" was wed in pomp and splendor, but sans the approval of the lady members of Denver's 400 of that day. If she felt the chill of this snub, she must have been warmed

IN THIS HOUSE Horace and Augusta lived during the years of his ascendancy. Bone of contention was her determination to remain in unostentatious home, opposing his desire to make more of a display of his ever-increasing wealth. Building at right is early-day assay office.

THE "MATCHLESS" MINE SHAFT opening is covered by grating. At left is cage with just room for man.

THE SHACK ON FRYER HILL where Baby Doe spent her last years and where her frozen body was found. The head house of the Matchless is at the left.

somewhat by her $7,000 bridal dress and the attendance of President Arthur and members of his cabinet.

Their first-born, Lillie, wore for her christening a creation costing $15,000.

A huge mansion rose to house the new family of the now soaring Horace Tabor, and it was surrounded by stables, parks and fountains with elegant statuary.

Tabor had disposed of his partnership holdings and owned scores of mines by himself. His income was more than $4,000,000 a year, and his "pet," the Matchless Mine, alone dumped $2,000 a day into his already bulging pockets.

Typical of his wild extravagances was the purchase of a yacht in New York, and by 1886, it was becoming apparent that even his fabulous income could not keep up with his expenditures. Singly and severally, his mines and other sources of income went into insolvency, failed, or were sold to satisfy creditors. The fabulous Tabor was back where he started.

Now, broken and nearly 70 years old, he went prospecting again for a year, enduring hardships as severe as those of his early days. Then he was given, as a small recognition of former generosities to his party, a job as postmaster in Denver. This he held only a little more than a year, when he died there.

Destitute, Baby Doe soon was forced to move to Leadville, and into the little cabin at the mouth of the Matchless. There she eked out a miserable existence, her daughters gone, one to marry and live elsewhere, and one to die under dubious conditions in a shabby roominghouse in Chicago. She walked down to Leadville at intervals to buy leftover scraps for food, her feet wrapped in gunny-sacks in winter. And, in the cabin, close to the Matchless she died, freezing and alone.

SAINT ELMO, COLORADO

Here is a little town to satisfy anyone. Its environs have fallen away, but this has only served to concentrate what is left into a sort of antique doll town. True, there are gaps, but the short stretch of street offers all that one would expect in an old western town; false fronts, tiny church, log cabins and all.

Several canyons come together here to feed Chalk Creek. Dense woods covered the site in 1878 and the tiny cluster of cabins was dignified by the name of Forrest City.

Soon the collection of houses boasted stores and hotels and was incorporated with a new name, Saint Elmo.

At first, while the population was limited to about 2,000, the town was of high moral tone. Church services were held every few months in one private residence or another when a visiting clegyman would pass that way.

As the place grew, however, it took on all the roistering aspects of a predominantly single male population, with saloons and dance halls going full tilt. Patrons were not only miners but railroad crews from towns below.

Though several camps were established farther up the canyons, notably Romley and Hancock, none surpassed Saint Elmo in size or weekend celebrations.

SAINT ELMO GIVES EFFECT of a town in miniature. Sky is heavily overcast. Moment of sun makes little false fronts stand out against darkly-timbered mountain.

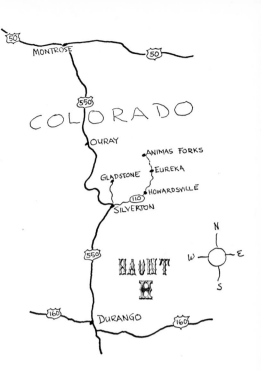

GHOSTLY MISTS OF THE MOUNTAINS

SILVERTON, COLORADO

Silverton is not a true Ghost Town, being on a main highway and the hub of an area containing many revived or continuing mining operations.

At the turn of the century it was the supply center, the "metropolitan" area, of a vast network of towns, mines and mills that had flourished in the gold and silver bonanza days of the 80's and 90's. Silverton, along with the rest of Colorado, was staggered by repeated blows in those years. The Federal Government had been buying 4,500,000 ounces of silver a month under the Sherman Act, and India's mints provided a huge outlet for the metal. But suddenly in 1893, India ceased coining silver money and shortly thereafter the Sherman Act was repealed. These events created panic in Colorado, and silver mining was never the same again.

Silverton is located in a "Park," a small area surrounded by towering peaks of the San Juan Range on one side and those of the La Plata Mountains on the other. The elevation is well over 9,000 feet and this means heavy snows for a long period in winter. The streets are lined with many buildings dating from those hectic days when Silver was King. Many are occupied and doing business in a quiet way.

The Denver Rio Grande Railroad still runs its diminutive train up here from Durango. This is the narrow-gauge train now famous for its role in the motion picture *Around the World in Eighty Days.*

The town is a center for trips to a good many deserted mining camps and towns, notably Eureka, Animas Forks and Gladstone.

EUREKA, COLORADO

Eureka is suffering more rapid erasure than results from mere decay. Its store buildings are mostly torn down, the lumber to be put to more active service in Silverton. There is now no main street in Eureka, which once boasted the "finest saloons anywhere." This pride in alcohol emporiums had been continuous since 1896 when, of the several buildings comprising Eureka, the "saloon was the finest."

The beginnings of the place were in 1860, when Baker, (for w h o m Baker's Park, the locale of Silverton, was named) and his party did some digging and panning in the banks of the rushing Animas River. Eureka was no boom-town, but grew slowly and steadily. The Sunnyside mill was easily the leader as a producer of income for the populace. There was even train service to Eureka, beginning in 1896.

Looked at from above, on the road continuing up the canyon, the town is seen to be situated on an "island" extending over the elbow formed by a curve in the river. This got the center of town out from under the terrific avalanches so c o m m o n in late winter, though fringe a r e a s were devastated.

When the Sunnyside mills closed in 1938, the town died. Now even the mill is gone. Only impressive foundations run up the steep mountainside as reminders of camp town glory days.

ON OUR WAY TO ANIMAS FORKS we come to a wider spot on the narrow steep road. Stopping to look back on Eureka it is easy to see why avalanches crashed down into the valley. Old mine sites are everywhere on precipitous slopes.

BUSINESS BUILDINGS are nearly gone. At left are foundations of giant Sunnyside Mill which produced $50,000,000 in gold, lead, silver, zinc and copper. Tram line is visible, as are tailings and mine heads.

HOMES OF MINERS cluster on tiny level area, far out as possible from steep sides of canyon. Small patch of snow is visible, though picture was made in July, was first of more and larger banks farther up defile leading to Animas Forks.

ANIMAS FORKS AND GLADSTONE, COLORADO

By the very nature of the reason for their existence, the old mining camps are often placed in spectacular situations. Among these, Animas Forks holds first place in our experience. Its elevation is 11,300 feet, with craggy, snowy peaks of over 13,000 feet rising in circles around the site. The roaring waters of the Animas leave the town and rush on down the gorge in a canyon, narrow and deep. The snow, even in July, is not restricted to the peaks, but lies in banks in every shaded corner of the town.

The canyon of the Animas is here so narrow that the original road was a real problem to build. And when the little narrow-gauge came in about 1898, there was no place to put it except on the road. Now the tracks and rails are long gone and the road restored.

The remaining buildings are scattered, but give some idea of the plan of the original streets. These were few because of the terrain.

Getting a good start in 1875, Animas Forks soon grew to be the "largest town in the world." The boast was followed by fine print reading "at this altitude."

Avalanches were the bane of the town, wiping out many buildings and frequently stopping travel up the river. Timber was stripped from the steep mountainsides to be used as fuel, shoring, etc. and this smoothed the way for sliding tons of snow. The sides of the canyon are so close together that the wave of snow would not halt at the bottom, but would roll part way up the other side, actually lifting the buildings off their foundations.

SOME OF HIGHEST PEAKS in Colorado tower above remnants of Animas Forks, even though town itself is over 11,000 feet high. Continental divide is in background, stream in foreground is Animas, near its beginning.

JAIL WAS STOUTLY constructed, every window offered spectacular view of San Juans. Structure is almost buried in snow most of year, brush and grass have three-month growing season.

At the farthest end of town were large mines and mills, and conveniently, a boardinghouse. In the kitchen stood a huge cookstove. Those miners no doubt packed healthy appetites! A nearby trap door led down a flight of stairs to what must have been a cold-storage vault. At this altitude and in the short summer, the pit could easily have been the equivalent of a deep freeze unit.

The large room adjoining the kitchen showed empty window sashes opening on an array of snowy peaks.

Here was frenzied activity during the 70's and 80's. Then most of the richer mines began to peter out, the mills closed down or moved downgrade to Eureka and all was quiet again.

From Animas Forks we descend to Eureka, then on down to Silverton, the "hub" of the mining area, and up Cement Creek to Gladstone. The stream is small and not spectacular, and its waters are stained red by iron.

At first Gladstone seems entirely deserted, but a mine on the mountainside is being operated again.

Not many buildings are left standing, but many evidences of foundations and mining equipment attest to those busy times in the 80's and 90's.

BEFORE THOS. WALSH became completely wrapped up in Camp Bird Mine over mountains near Ouray he had interests in Silverton, Eureka and Animas Forks. This was his home. Daughter Evelyn grew up to merge fortune with that of the McLeans and as Evelyn Walsh McLean ruled Washington society, dabbled in politics and sported sinister Hope diamond.

GLOWERING CLOUDS hanging on peaks of Rockies allow shafts of light to gleam on few remaining buildings of Gladstone.

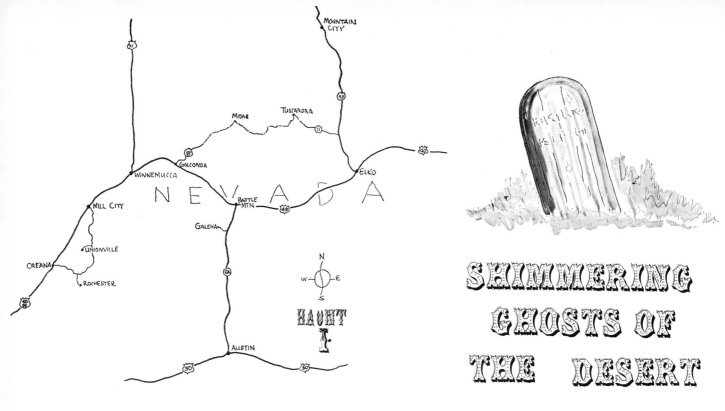

SHIMMERING GHOSTS OF THE DESERT

UNIONVILLE, NEVADA

Spence Davidson, one of the residents along the creek, allows he arrived in town "quite a while ago!" He gives some data on Unionville.

"Quite a while ago" turned out to be 1890. "Was the town busy then?" "No, it was really dead even then; it had an early start, about 1860." Unionville saw only about ten really good, boom years, and was almost finished by 1880. In this brief period the place had undergone sudden expansion, with 20 new people moving in every day at first. These new residents soon needed, first, nine saloons; then 10 stores, an express office, livery stables and, at the fringe, the inevitable red light district. The girls of the cribs at first did very well, but many families moved to Unionville which, with its water and shade, offered more comforts than starker camps. The proportion of single men shrank and so did the "houses."

But the schools grew, and today the best preserved building is the one on the hill, facing the town. Several ranchers in the valley had as many as six children and these kept the school going until a few years ago. The last teacher was Mrs. Hammersmark, a sister-in-law of Mr. Davidson. She passed away recently in Reno.

Unionville, by virtue of its quick expansion, in the early 70's had become the seat of the then Humboldt County. The Courthouse was in a rented saloon in its early years. During Unionville's period of activity, it had produced some $3,000,000, largely in silver. The Arizona mine above the town had been the big one, with more than a third of the total to its credit.

IN THE 70's STEADY STREAMS of customers poured though doors of Unionville "Emporium." Stone is local and varied in color, making beautiful effect.

Close by are the ruins of a small mill, and close to them the opening of the gold mine. From this cavern bursts a torrent of air of about 50 degrees, startlingly luxurious in the noonday heat of the Humboldt Foothills.

The cemetery on the way to the main road is large, but with many headboards missing. Those remaining mostly bear dates in the 70's, when the population had reached its peak of some 2,000 to 3,000. Many graves are enclosed in the usual ornate wooden fences. There certainly is a much larger population here now than in Unionville itself.

BUENA VISTA SCHOOL has not sheltered pupils for years but is in good condition. Heating stove stands in center, surrounded by desks graduated in size for different grades. Map of Africa on wall was made in 1887.

HOLES IN FALSE FRONT show where birds are nesting. Scraps of sheet metal have preserved building beyond life of others, warding off weather and sparks of neighboring fires.

ROCHESTER, NEVADA

Rochester is all "uphill," with the center of town occupying the only nearly level area. This is the "old town." A somewhat newer, less picturesque Rochester is first encountered at a lower level.

In what was the business section of upper Rochester only one building still stands erect. It is a typical false front of the day, once the Post Office combined with a store and living quarters.

The little sliding window for dispensing eagerly awaited mail opens from a room filled with debris. Here is an old brass bedstead, and on it a moldy mattress. For a cover it has a motheaten sheepskin coat. Also on the bed is a little booklet, tattered and stained, titled "How to Play the Zither."

All around this building are many foundations and basements giving support to the town's history of 1,500 people. That was at the height of the period between 1860 and 1913. Over all, some $10,000,000 worth of silver was produced. As usual, other metals were a by-product, sometimes paying for the cost of production.

Above the main part of town are extensive mine dumps and ruins of head-buildings. Here also are the remains of a large building, recently collapsed, that must have been a saloon and dance hall on the grand scale. Broken tables are overturned everywhere, as are chairs and carved counters. A prone stairway once led upstairs to pleasures other than gambling, an expected adjunct to any drinking place of that day.

MIDAS, NEVADA

When the populace petitioned for a Post Office in 1908 the desired name was "Gold Circle." The powers that be, however, looked on this name with about as much favor as they had for Raw Dog, Oregon, but for different reasons. There were already too many Gold this and Gold thats in Nevada, so how about "Midas" which, after all, did have a golden touch?

Original discoveries had been made the year before and the town became a reality shortly after. It grew apace, though not with the resounding boom that was being enjoyed at the same time by Goldfield and others. Estimates of peak population vary from 5,000 to 20,000. This will allow a safe margin for errors. There was a Chamber of Commerce, city water system, a newspaper, four big general stores and several hotels and rooming houses. In addition, there existed the usual shady area, dotted at night with red lights, and numerous saloons.

The big mine in Midas was the Elko Prince. About 1910, miners were forced to accept part of their wages in stock, times were so hard, but some sold later for as much as 500 per cent gain.

The Post Office, always a barometer of a town's population closed in 1942 along with the gold mines, the school in 1952, lacking the three pupils required by law to keep it going.

PEACEFUL IS THE WORD now for Main Street in Midas. Little store at right carried everything from corsets to kerosene.

TUSCARORA, NEVADA

Nearing Tuscarora one first sees the cemetery, its white headstones and boards conspicuous against the gray-green sage and brown earth. Then comes the red brick smelter stack so noticeable on the hill above the town.

It is surprising to see a little stream of ice cold water running right across the road. How blessed was Tuscarora! Among Nevada mining camps few had an abundance of good water. Not that the miners cared much for the stuff for drinking. And Tuscarora had no wish to be unique, its population imbibing more whiskey than water. It was as wild and rip-roaring a camp as any, and worse than some. Its biggest decades were from 1870 to 1890 when several thousand whites and two thousand Chinese kept excitement going.

The Chinese came to build the Central Pacific Railroad and remained to dispense opium in a dark underground section of the town, concealed by an innocent looking China Town. For a time at least, they also ran most of the brothels and gambling joints. Some of these were behind and under laundries and others brazenly exposed, with red lights hanging at the doors of the cribs.

The town of the euphonius name and beautiful situation on Mount Blitzen produced $40,000,000, in silver mostly, so it must have buckled down to work daytimes.

VAULT SEEMS TO INDICATE ruins might have been bank. Under many respectable buildings in Tuscarora were opium dens, other houses of vice.

GALENA, NEVADA

What remains of this once bustling gold camp forms a satisfying ghostly remnant. Complete desertion is the lot of Galena, where once the population surpassed that of the nearby metropolis, Battle Mountain.

It was laid out in 1869 and in a couple of years had burgeoned into a boom town complete with a park, a rarity in a day when more thought was given to roistering than to the beauties of nature. The most conspicuous feature of Galena, though, was the smelter built to extract silver and lead from the rough material produced by the Dutch Creek Mine. This amounted to some $5,000,000.

The mill itself has long since disappeared, but its site is marked by extensive tailings dumps. These are constituted of flour-fine material which has solidified into piles of something like hard clay. Above these are dumps of waste rock, each heap a different color, the native material being so varied from place to place.

The cemetery is quite large. The earlier dates still discernible on the old headboards are in the 70's. It is close to town, the equivalent of a couple of blocks, and those who died with their boots on were simply carried over and buried with little ceremony. A bottle was passed around afterward, and that was that.

IF THIS WAS "PUBLIC SQUARE," perhaps tiny band played Sousa here on summer evenings, as was the custom in so many towns of era.

MAIN STREET IS SPARSELY fringed by scattered structures. Upper, with fancy railing likely was boardinghouse. Rock in street is mostly galena ore, some glittering with silver, lead.

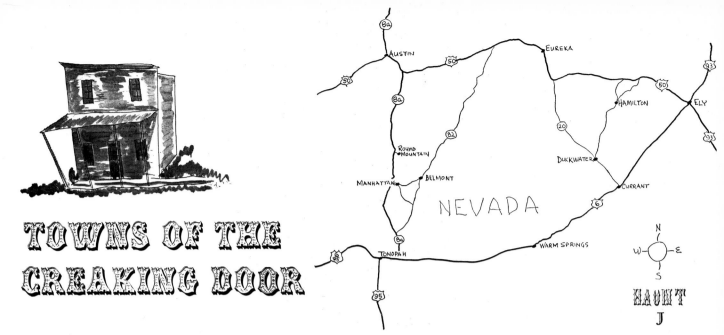

TOWNS OF THE CREAKING DOOR

NEVADA

N
W · E
S

HAUNT
J

EUREKA, NEVADA

Eureka, in 1864, was all set for the explosive rush and boom of other mining camps. Certainly the discovery of lead-silver deposits was as spectacular and important as most, and one of the first big finds of the bi-metallic ore in the country. But expansion of the infant settlement was slowed by the refractory qualities of the material. New methods of smelting had to be devised. The first plant built in 1869 was a failure. Another was erected with different, hitherto unknown grinders and baking methods. This was more successful and pointed the way to still better ways of extracting the metal. Then the boom began in earnest and by 1880 Eureka's population had reached nearly 10,000. But then

OBVIOUSLY NOT A "DEAD" ghost town, Eureka is a museum of mining history. The Main Street, coinciding with the highway, is lively with stores, fire department and other establishments. Balcony of theatre offered cooling breezes during intermissions, was not so popular in winter.

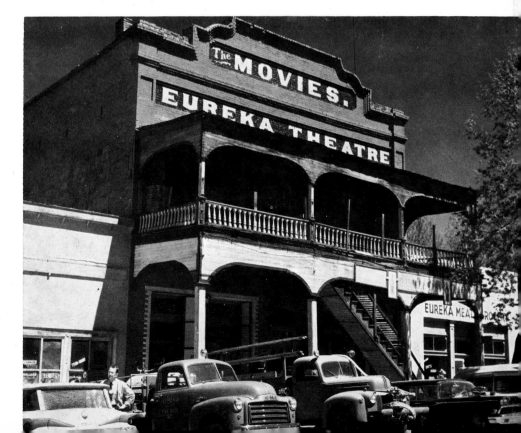

production began to fall off and things looked bad for the young town. About this time several Comstock-made millionaires built a railroad into Eureka, and because of its central position in the state, the town became a railhead for the whole area.

But the mining boom was over, to revive weakly at intervals, in 1905, during the first world war and in the 30's. The smelters, established under such difficulties, had been closed since 1891. Stamp mills, cyanide plants, refineries and smelters have always meant as much to the economy of these early camps as the actual mining operations. Their end means slow strangulation and such was the case for Eureka. However, there is still life here, partly due to the fact that a paved highway with its tourists passes through. Eureka deserves a day or so of looking around, for it is full of historic buildings, ruins of smelters and mementos of the days when it produced $40,000,000 in silver, $20,000,000 in gold and 225,000 pounds of lead.

AUSTIN, NEVADA

Austin is one of those historic old mining camps that would be a true Ghost Town but for the highway running through it.

OLD MAIN STREET of Austin is quiet now, except for some bars, and even these do not approach the glitter of some in other cities of Nevada. Catholic church dominates skyline.

OUTSIDE STAIRWAY IS richly reminiscent of early days in Austin and Eureka. It led to balcony where the populace lolled on warm summer evenings, also served as access to upper floors of building.

Old brick buildings with collapsed walls and ruins of adobe structures alternate along the street with small stores and gambling houses. The "one-armed bandits" have replaced the real thing in Austin, and probably receive a much larger "take."

The history of Austin began when, in 1862, a horse kicked up a piece of quartz, laced with gold. The owner of the horse was W. H. Talbott and he sent the specimen to Virginia City for assay. Finding that there was silver as well as gold in it, he staked out his claim, others followed, and a silver rush was on.

The locality was inaccessible, but miners and would-be claim owners helped build a road, receiving city lots in exchange.

A brick courthouse was built in 1869, Austin having become the county seat in September of 1863, when some 10,000 people swarmed the town. Already a lumber mill was going full tilt and more than four hundred houses had been built. By the time the courthouse was in use there were many other "permanent" structures including schools, three churches, several hotels, stores and the usual quota of saloons and red light houses.

Austin was composed of so many brick and adobe buildings, clay being more plentiful than lumber, that it suffered somewhat less from fires than did other camps. But floods, especially those of 1868 and 1874, ravaged it.

By 1880 Austin had started the downhill slide and most of its total of $50,000,000 in ore was an accomplished fact.

The railroad, result of so much hard work to acquire, was abandoned in 1938, and this really was the finish of the town as a mining center.

Austin, once so hard to reach, now one of the most accessible of the old camps, is comparatively unspoiled and well worth the study of those interested in the bonanza day of the Old West.

HAMILTON, NEVADA

Hardly a more wind-swept, storm-raked, altogether desolate landscape could be imagined than the one on the slope of White Pine Mountain in 1865. The only living things were the rabbits, squirrels, snakes, owls and other desert creatures.

In that year a group of prospectors from Austin found rich silver deposits there. They banded together with other Austin men of more wealth to form the Monte Cristo Mining Company. The whole thing was kept as quiet as possible and for several years not much happened.

Then, on a bitter cold, stormy day in January 1868 a nearly solid silver deposit was found on Treasure Hill, just across the bowl-shaped hollow in which lay the beginnings of Hamilton. This set off one of those fabulous "rushes" during which people of every sort and description poured into the snowy, inhospitable town which burgeoned till it burst at the seams. Jerry-built and substantial structures rose side by side. A new county was created, "White Pine," a courthouse rose almost overnight. This was used largely as a place to settle constant litigation over conflicting claims.

By now the rabbits were displaced by 25,000 humans scattered over the several ridges contiguous to Hamilton. These people ran the gamut from respectable, hard-working men down to the ever present hangers-on, the sharpies and prostitutes. Several houses for the latter lined a short street near the edge of town.

At 8,000 feet elevation the climate was rigorous, there was no local water, food had to be freighted in from Elko and bandits waylaid the lines of stages and pack mules going out. But the dream of El Dorado sustained the populace. Wasn't the silver lying around in almost pure chunks?

One of the largest and most imposing buildings erected was the Withington Hotel, built of sandstone and Oregon pine and indeed a structure to endure forever.

Then from here and there in small, quiet voices began to come doubts that the silver went very deep, that when the shining surface deposits were scraped off, the future of Hamilton would be something less than the rosy picture painted by the newspapers of the town.

And these voices of gloom were right; the silver was all on top. By 1873 there was a noticeable drop in output. There was a leveling-off process of a few years with small spurts upward, bigger ones downward. In spite of all the glittering prophecies in the early years, 1887 saw the end of the big-scale production. By then there had been shipped out a total of some $22,000,000 in bullion.

RUINS OF Withington hotel dominate Hamilton.

People moved away almost as fast as they had poured in. The "birds of prey" went first, to fatten in other, newer camps.

Before many years the town was completely deserted, the buildings fell into disrepair, then ruin. There were two disastrous fires. Stone structures crumbled.

About twenty frame and stone stores and houses remain pitifully scattered about the hollow. Traces of wooden sidewalks partly connect some of them.

DOORWAY OF WITH-INGTON HOTEL laid open to elements frames group of houses almost isolated by past fires.

MANHATTAN, NEVADA

The town called Manhattan Gulch in early days lay almost on the slopes of Bald Mountain at an altitude of nearly 7,000 feet. This means heavy snows for a long winter, and Manhattan really had them. The ground was out of sight for many months, most winters, with hot summers between.

This sort of climate didn't prevent a hectic boom in the period from 1900 to 1905.

Nearly forgotten is the earlier period of activity there in the 60's. That first stage in the camp's growth was short, and from about 1890 until John C. Humphrey came upon his dazzling chunk of "Jewelry Ore," the town had slumbered. The few people still there awoke with a start at this discovery and so did a lot of opportunists throughout Nevada.

When Charles Phillips, now of Portland, was born there in 1910, Manhattan was a busy place, with about 500 people. Charles was only ten years old when he left with his parents, going to Goldfield, but he has many memories of the town in the Gulch.

"WE WENT TO RIPPY'S Grocery for almost everything, besides food. We went in by door on the corner, I remember." Native of Manhattan, Charles Phillips, says proprietor and family lived upstairs. Route to "outhouse" went down, then up.

"There were several mines going strong in that period," he recalled. "The largest was the White Caps, with its stamp mill and cyanide plant. The La Verde and Big Four also milled their own ore, all of it gold. I remember the White Caps pumped its seepage water into the gulch, water so full of arsenic it was useless. Too bad, since water was so scarce.

"Some of the main buildings along the main street were Oliver Giannini's Saloon, Ziegler's Butcher Shop, Ferguson's Drugstore and Butler's Livery Stable. The jail was close to the stone post office.

"The mule skinners used to throw whatever came handy at their refractory animals, and these missiles were often 'high grade.' I've heard since, that during the depression days, a man and his wife harvested these chunks and sold them for a tidy sum. Those were mostly $5.00 rocks!

"I remember a character who made his living at 'dry placering,' a process using air instead of water. He was called 'Dry Wash Wilson' and had the largest feet ever seen in that part of Nevada. He realized a dream of many years when he bought a 1910 Model T Ford. But his happiness turned to gloom when he found he couldn't put his foot on just one pedal at a time.

The town now can hardly muster up 20 people, some remain from the small-sized resurgence in the 30's. Most are about ready to admit theirs is a Ghost Town, with small hopes for revival. A few feel that if the price of gold would advance, "something good might happen to Manhattan!"

CATHOLIC CHURCH commands imposing position on hill above town. Interior is empty except for altar rail and confessional.

POST OFFICE WAS FOCAL point of all activity; when mail came into town, everybody picked up his own. Jail stood almost against building and was usually well filled with drunks sobering up.

BELMONT, NEVADA

Belmont's history was hectic and brief, with only about twenty frenzied years allotted as the life span for the city. In that time Belmont became the seat of Nye County and produced $15,000,000 worth of lead and silver ore. There were spasmodic bursts of enthusiasm at intervals after the boom period was ended in 1885. Discovery of turquoise in 1909 caused a flurry, but this was short lived. A 100-ton flotation mill was built in 1914 with bright hopes and almost the entire resources of its promoters, but after a couple of years it failed. Another stamp mill was built in 1921 but suffered the same fate in less time.

The Nye County Courthouse, built in 1867 dominates the town, an interesting and picturesque structure. A few feet from the imposing front door is a small stream meandering across the grass-grown street.

In common with other early day mining camps the place saw its difficulties between miners, owners and the unions. Two of the union organizers found such a complete lack of welcome that they were forced to flee. Unfortunately they didn't go far enough, holing up in a mine tunnel near town. Here they were caught, dragged into town and hanged on the main street. One was only a boy of 15.

Across the street from the spot where this brutal episode took place stands one of the most interesting of old-time buildings, the Music Hall, and across the front in old-style lettering is its name, fading but brave, the "Cosmopolitan." Once garishly red and green, time has subdued the brilliance of its paint, and warped its boards to curls. Flagstones, split from nearby rocks, pave its outdoor foyer, under the extending balcony. Remains of fancy lace curtains hang from glass upstairs windows and weeds and sage grow in the doorway. An iron ring to which the driver tied his horse while the star stepped from her carriage, still hangs on one of the posts supporting the balcony.

DESERTED MAIN STREET sees little traffic now, but once was busy parade of buggies, ore wagons and people in costumes of period from 60's and through gay 90's.

MONITOR-BELMONT MILL is almost gone but stack of smelter stands as monument.

CENTER OF ALL PUBLIC entertainment in bustling era of Belmont's heyday was "Cosmopolitan." Music hall dominated street.

LIFE OF IMPOSING NYE County Courthouse extended from 1867 to 1905. Building had no "central heating"; rooms were heated by stoves connected to many chimneys. Even jail at rear had its own.

ACROSS FROM "COSMOPOLITAN" stands group of typical mining camp buildings. Here were hanged labor organizer and youthful companion. Street becomes road leading down hill to Monitor-Belmont Mill.

ONCE "IMPREGNABLE" JAIL, now open-air affair, is extension of courthouse.

TONOPAH, NEVADA

The story of the Mizpah Mine and its discovery has been told in several forms, but the most likely version is the one in which William Hall tried to boot his partner, Jim Butler, out of his blankets one spring morning in 1900, and failed. They had started from Butler's ranch on a trip to Southern Klondyke, a small mining camp. Fifteen miles short of their objective they came to Tonapah Springs and camped there.

Next morning, the early-rising Hall unable to rouse Butler, went on alone disgusted. In his own good time Butler arose, only to find his burros had "vamoosed" over the ridge. After tracking them down, he was pretty much out of sorts and picked up a rock to heave at them, but held on to it, not out of consideration for his beasts, but because the stone was flecked with mineral.

After locating the vein's source, he caught his burros and hurried to overtake his partner. Nothing much was happening in Southern Klondyke, however, and the partners soon returned to Belmont, gathering a few more samples at Tonopah Springs on the way.

It was Butler's wife who really started the ball rolling. She enlisted expert help in the person of Tasker L. Oddie, who was to figure prominently in Tonopah's subsequent history. Oddie, for an interest in the stake, had assays run proving the value of the samples would run $350 per ton.

Mrs. Butler staked a claim near Oddie's, naming it the Mizpah. This was one of the richest producers in the entire area.

There followed the usual influx; the sudden boom. Streets were laid out by Walter Gayhart, who saw fit to make his money in real estate rather than the sweaty job of mining.

Tonopah's heyday was the period centered about 1905, when it wrested the County Seat from Belmont. By 1913 there were definite signs that things were not going too well, and before long the big days were finished, having seen the production of $250,000,000 in gold and silver.

Tonopah is not dead, however. Some mining still goes on. The main street, flanked by the five-story Mizpah Hotel and many clubs, stores and restaurants, is still busy. Features of the town are the high curbs on each side. They rise to the height of about three feet and preclude stepping up just anywhere. The purpose of these is to channel the flood waters of frequent "gulley-washers" that pour through town.

The area is a veritable gem field, full of petrified wood, jasper and other semi-precious material.

STORM BUILDS UP over Tonopah. Town is at base of Mt. Oddie (right) whose sides and summit are eroded by diggings.

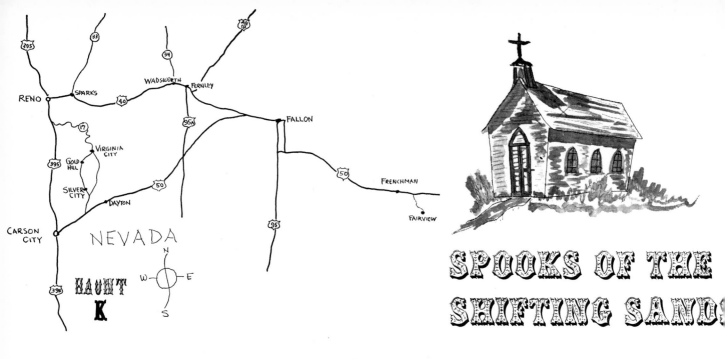

VIRGINIA CITY, NEVADA

Virginia City is among the best known of the old camps. The town is neither dead nor abandoned, but nevertheless it is popularly considered a ghost town.

It is situated almost on top of a mountain, offering spreading views of the Nevada terrain in several directions. It has larger buildings than most and more of them. It has as interesting history as any, and since it has never been completely abandoned, most of the past has been preserved in print. The delver into the story of Virginia City can spend days or weeks among relics, books and newspapers on display on the spot where it all happened.

MANY BUILDINGS in Virginia City retain charm of early days.

ORIGINAL ATMOSPHERE still exists away from "C" Street.

IMPRESSIVE RELIC is Fourth Ward School. Located near south end of town on "C" St., it once provided vantage point from which to view spectacular cave-in across street. Sizable area collapsed into cavern created by mines which honeycomb ground under city.

BRICK BUILDING IS often called John Mackay residence. Structure was actually union mine office. Mr. Mackay did stay here whenever he visited Virginia City on business.

ST. MARY'S IN THE MOUNTAINS.

BACK STREETS OF CITY look much as they did in heyday. The Knights of Pythias building is on the left. The building in the center housed Louis Schoenfeld's furniture store from 1864 to 1879. Unlike most furniture stores of the period, it was not combined with an undertaking parlor. Schoenfeld later moved to Seattle, Washington, where he founded the Standard Furniture, a branch of which in Tacoma is still operated by grandsons Herb and Ralph. On the right the Miners Union Hall stands unchanged except that balcony of latter is no longer safe vantage point from which to watch goings on in Virginia City.

ONE OF CHIEF GLORIES remaining of old Virginia City is St. Mary's in the Mountains. Building was completed in 1877, succeeding earlier church destroyed by fire of 1875. Bell is of Comstock silver.

DAYTON, NEVADA

Adolph Sutro was a "man with a dream" who conceived the idea of a horizontal tunnel so as to haul out the ore and drain off the water from the deepest shafts of the Comstock, whose mouths opened up near the top of Mt. Davidson, the site of Virginia City.

Almost insurmountable obstacles were placed in his way, especially financial ones. The big mining companies agreed to put up the huge sum of $5,000,000 and the money was eventually forthcoming in the shape of royalties of $2.00 per ton, the water to be free.

Delays stalled completion for thirteen years, so long that the heyday of the Comstock was over. Ore removal continued for years, however, and in 1880, as a sample year, the 20,489 feet of tunnel delivered two billion gallons of water; water almost impossible to remove vertically, which flooded mining operations and was so hot it steamed.

Dayton now has a charming old-time atmosphere with a good many of the original buildings standing here and there. It is not quite dead, however. Complete demise is impossible for any town on a highway. There will, at least, be filling stations and taverns.

YEARS HAVE PASSED since services were held in little church in Dayton. Graceful architecture is evident in doorway. Old church is separated from center of town which offers a typical group of early-day buildings.

FAIRVIEW, NEVADA

Fairview did not want to stay put; it pulled up stakes twice. The first location was no doubt settled upon because of unlimited level ground on which to build. The view from the site is a magnificent, endless expanse of desert backed up by equally arid mountains. One of these, nearer than the others, has two humps on its low summit. Naturally, the mine gouged out on its side was called "The Dromedary."

The most imposing structure built on site No. 1 was the bank, which included a solid stone and concrete vault. That there were many streets of houses and buildings to shelter and serve the 2,000 people who lived there, is attested by rows of cellars open to the skies. It seems the populace grew weary of commuting so far to the mines and mills, so they moved everything except the bank vault to a spot in the narrow canyon a couple of miles nearer the working area. The ancient vault, standing as the only monument to mark the abandoned location, can easily be seen from the highway.

After a few years in the constricted defile of porphyry rock, the new town again grew restive. Not finding enough space for expansion it was getting longer and longer with the width limited to one block.

So the third and final move was to gather around the mill, and here remain the vestiges of Fairview, its perambulations now long ended.

RAMBLING LITTLE "MAIN STREET" is remaining nucleus of once extensive town. Building at lower right once housed nice flock of chickens, but food for them proved difficult to provide. Buildings at left hold variety of ancient cars. Sagebrush on hills is almost evenly spaced, limited by scarcity of moisture.

LITTLE STRUCTURE HAS BEEN lonely home for Strattons 45 years. Rain barrels are hopefully lined up. When all are filled, couple feels secure. Since this is not often, Ed and Sylvia had to dispense with any form of livestock. Worn chopping blocks have seen hard service for many years.

ONCE PROUD "Bank of Fairview." Only useful purpose now is "Guest House," sheltering rare overnight guests.

THE KINDLY AND HOSPITABLE Strattons, Ed and Sylvia. She can see visitors approaching from afar; usually manages a spotless dress and white shoes before their arrival. Little house is filled with exquisite examples of fancywork, embroidery, crochet, tatting. "I have lots of time for it," she says.

Couple has lived in isolated mountain aerie since 1914, most of that time as only residents. Every six weeks or so they drive the 50 miles to nearest town, Fallon, in ancient car. They gather up accumulated mail, spend several days "living it up," stock up on groceries, head for home.

HAUNT L

WRAITHS OF THE WAILING WINDS

CANDELARIA, NEVADA

"Patrick O'Leary, Native of Ireland, Age 25 yrs." So reads an old headboard in the desolate cemetery on a sunbaked knoll above Candelaria.

Patrick sleeps in a setting far different from his cool, green Emerald Isle. There is no grass; no trees shade the little plot filled only with leaning headboards, blistering rocks and rattlesnakes.

Candelaria never had a Chamber of Commerce to boost it as a good place to live. It wouldn't have done any good, anyway. There were several livery stables with big piles of horse manure in back. The flies multiplied by millions and had free access to screenless windows of houses, hotels and boardinghouses.

All water was hauled from a spring nine miles away and cost those who used the stuff a dollar a gallon; whiskey was cheaper!

Even the stampmill dispensed with water in the crushers and the resultant pall of dust settled in the lungs of the miners, who died by dozens of "miner's consumption." Perhaps poor young Patrick O'Leary was one of those.

Mexicans had found silver ore here in 1864, but siesta prevailed until 1879, when a polyglot population of Germans, Slavonians and others, mostly foreign born, took over and built a boom town. Construction was largely of adobe and stone. At this time the big producer was the Northern Belle, credited with a $15,000,000 production in silver.

A narrow-gauge railroad, the Carson and Colorado, connected Candelaria to Keeler on the shores of Owens Lake (which once lay at the foot of Mt. Whitney) and to Mina. Other small towns sprang up along the line; Sodaville, Belleville, and more, but these are nearly gone by now.

After the first big silver boom the town nearly died, breathing only fitfully until about the turn of the century when it revived to the tune of some $1,000,000 worth of gold, lead and copper, along with more silver.

FORTRESS-LIKE STONE STRUCTURE had varied career. It served as a bank, was almost impregnable during raids by bandits and holdup men. Stores, saloons and other business ventures shared quarters at different times. Interior seems dark in contrast to glare of outdoors, windows were purposely omitted as offering weak spots to attack.

HOT SUN SIMMERS GRAVEYARD. Grave enclosures were common in early cemeteries. Ornamentation differed on each. In this picture the one at left protects the grave of Patrick O'Leary. Main street of Candelaria extends beyond. Extensive stamp mills were at point where road curves to left in distance. Most mines were on hill at left, just out of camera range.

LAST YEARS OF SPASMODIC ACTIVITY developed several dugouts to augment vanishing buildings and to escape extremes of climate. Name "Candelaria" signifies the Day of Candlemas, anniversary of Mary's taking the Infant Jesus to the temple; was chosen by devout early Mexican prospectors. Significance was soon forgotten.

EVEN THE TREES ARE pallid ghosts. Picket fence enclosed house, vanished long ago.

GOLD POINT, NEVADA

The town really boasts only one group of store buildings dating from the earliest days, the typical tiny structures huddling together, putting on a brave show of false fronts and gingerbread. A couple of blocks above is the Post Office, apparently abandoned. A sign, once hung over it, is now on its side on the porch; it reads *"Gold Point, Nevada live population (so far) 28. Ghost unlimited. Altitude 5,800. Taxes very low."* At *this* date 28 would be a high estimate, less than half that number still live in the Gold Point area.

Originally christened "Hornsilver," it went along with the title until 1929. At that time silver had so languished that investors decided that "Gold Point" would have more value as a name.

Two thousand people once thronged the streets, which provided the usual saloons, hotels and stores, now dwindled to our forlorn little huddle and some scattered shacks.

Poor milling processes in those days which lost most of the values in the tailings, together with constant litigation over rights of the mill to operate, killed the town. It slumbers now, awaiting the resurrection.

GOLD POINT NEARS END of yet another day. Desert landscape stretches beyond, its Joshua trees and buttes soon to merge into darkness.

GOLDFIELD, NEVADA

In the center of Goldfield is a large hotel.   Although all its doors are padlocked, in the lobby there is a grand piano surrounded by leather "settees," and luxurious chairs.

In the dining room everything is set up for a normal, busy dinner hour.   Leather-backed chairs are drawn up to the tables spread with linen covers.   Silver, glasses and sugar bowl await the diner.   Only the heavy mantle of dust gives evidence that these tables had been set up long ago for a repast never served.

Goldfield is dead.   This is a city once boasting a population of 30,000 where, in the boom of 1906, lots sold for $45,000.   Originally called "Grandpa" when Billy March and Harry Stimler staked out their claim in 1902, the name was changed when "jewelry rock" running $50 to $100 a pound was found.

There were plenty of labor troubles, strikes and disorders of all sorts.   Several times State Police troops had to be called in to restore order, an uneasy quiet at best.   High grading was common and almost unsuppressed.   Miners put rich blosssom rocks heavily laced with gold in their pockets and lunch boxes, peddling them to waiting fences at night.

Uncounted saloons flourished in Goldfield, the most famous one, Tex Rickard's Northern, had a bar so long 80 tenders were necessary.

Tex Rickard made his fortune in the Klondike, lost it in California, and came to

GOLDFIELD HOTEL puts up brave front but shelters no guests.

Goldfield with the gold strike. His first big promotion was the champion prize fight between Gans and Nelson in 1906. That fight lasted 42 rounds, and put Gans up as the world lightweight champion.

The all-time high in production was $11,000,000, but this phenomenal figure dropped to $5,000,000 by 1912, and those who recognized the signs began to pull out. In 1918 the mines put out only $1,500,000 and this was cut in half the next year. The next three together saw only $150,000 produced. Then even this dwindled and Goldfield joined the ranks of has-beens, but probably few Ghost Towns put on such an impressive front of buildings standing and in good repair. It takes a second look to discern the boarded-up windows, the bars across the doors, the padlocks and nails barring the way into once-busy buildings and stores. The corpse "looks so natural."

RHYOLITE, NEVADA

Towering concrete remnants, dazzling white in the sun, are what is left of a city that expanded almost beyond belief from the day in 1904, when Eddie Cross and the renowned "Shorty" Harris discovered their rich specimen of ore. It was a sample of what the "Bullfrog Mine" to-be would produce, until its collapse such a brief period later.

Here is a depot with no train or tracks, and the vestiges of a school built for an expected population explosion which fizzled. The first school had been ludicrously inadequate, falling far short of holding the juvenile element by the time it was finished. So

MAIN STREET OF RHYOLITE leads past remains of one of the biggest booms in all history. The school, its future grossly overestimated, stands forlornly in ruins at lower end of street.

the next was conceived and planned on a grandiose scale. It was used only a short time and was never filled.

The panic of 1907 shattered dreams that did not have time to become reality. Succeeding financial difficulties, foreclosures, withdrawals of public utilities and pinching out of veins battered at the city whose concrete buildings were newly finished.

By 1910 Rhyolite's 10,000 people had dwindled to a few hundred, then to a few dozen. For years only two buildings have been tenable; the depot and a unique structure made of bottles. These are occupied, and serve as museums. The city that was the "Gem of the Amargosa" is otherwise deserted.

STEPS LEAD THROUGH front door of bank into shambles of concrete remnants of once-flourishing concern.

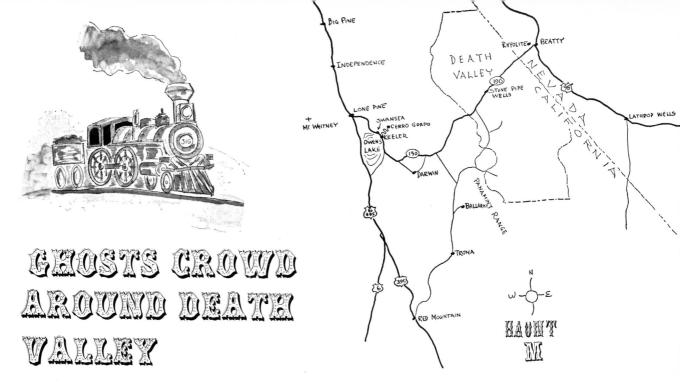

GHOSTS CROWD AROUND DEATH VALLEY

DARWIN, CALIFORNIA

A group of emaciated, weary men had negotiated fearful stretches of desert and mountains and were camped in the Argus Range. They were hungry and nearly exhausted. The last straw was the discovery that the sight was missing from the only serviceable gun and the killing of any game seemed impossible. An Indian guide, a native to the region, said he could fix the gun, took the weapon and disappeared into the hills. Before long he returned with it. The gun had a new sight of pure silver!

At this point, the main object was to reach the haven of the San Joaquin valley, but the thought of the native silver from which that gun sight had been made stayed with some of the group.

Years later, one Darwin French headed an expedition into the Argus Mountains to search out the lost "Gun Sight Mine." It was never found, but the party did locate mineral deposits worth investigating, and a camp was set up to start mining operations. While Darwin French was the exploring type, not a miner, and soon departed, the embryo town took the name of Darwin and as such developed into a lusty young giant with all the trappings, the saloons, red light houses and roisterous goings-on characteristic of those days.

FIRST SCHOOL IN Darwin was built with funds raised by "passing the hat."

CERRO GORDO, CALIFORNIA

The town's mineral wealth was first discovered in 1865 by Mexican prospectors, who applied the name, "Cerro Gordo." Literally translated, this means "Fat Hill."

For two years not much happened, then one of its discoverers showed a few chunks of silver ore to some mining men in Virginia City. That did it. Los Angeles, a small dying cattle town, received one of the first loads of bullion and revived suddenly.

The moving force to get things going at Cerro Gordo needed something more dynamic than the siesta-taking Mexican pioneers. Mortimer W. Belshaw provided the required spark. He had studied engineering and knew just how to do it. He took over the Union Mine which was producing the lead he needed for smelting. Machinery for smelters was hauled in and lifted over cliffs with an ingenious block and tackle system. A road was built and water piped in.

Ore was hauled to the bottom of the grade where a town named Keeler sprang up as a terminus. This was located on the shore of a large lake reflecting the highest part of the Sierra. Owens Lake is gone now, but the steamboats, *Bessie Brady* and *Molly Stevens,* made regular trips across it in those days. The terminal on the far shore, at the very foot of the Sierra, was Cartago. Next the precious stuff went to San Pedro. All this cost more than $50.00 a ton, so development of smelters on the spot was well worth while.

Cerro Gordo had more than its share of violence. For a time there were almost weekly shootings. The daily six-horse stage was frequently held up. So were the wagons hauling Belshaw's "Long Loaves," 85-pound slabs of precious metal from the local smelters intended for the U.S. Mint.

ALMOST ALL THAT IS left of Cerro Gordo is shown here. At extreme left, ruins of upper terminus of tram house, next (in back) is "Waterfall, Gilded House of Pleasure," at right of road (in repair) was residence of big wheel, M. W. Belshaw. Right, in front, is American House Hotel, lower center is livery stable. Above all tower tailings dumps of main shaft, mine head buildings are concealed behind them.

BALLARAT, CALIFORNIA

The names of our old towns, and why they were selected, are interesting facets of history.

Cornucopia is often used, signifying the horn of plenty. Bonanza, Fairview and White Hills are obvious in origin. But Ballarat?

Research shows that gold was discovered in Australia two years after California's big find of 1849. The discovery was made in Ballarat, Victoria, in the southeast part of the country down under. And it was at Ballarat, Australia, in 1869, that the largest nugget in the world was found. It weighed an incredible 2,284 ounces.

The hopeful founders of this California desert town must have baptized it (with whiskey, of course) "Ballarat" for the famous one in Australia. Prospectors, in the 1890's, discovered the yellow metal in several of the canyons leading out of the western flank of the Panamint Mountains.

HOUSE MELTS SLOWLY into earth from which it sprang. View is away from mountains looking east across blazing desert. Dry lake shows as white streak behind shack. Tiny tin-roofed house was home of lonely prospector until fairly recent years.

The Panamint Valley, mostly a glaring white, dry lake bed, butts up against the steeply rising Panamints. These culminate in Telescope Peak, 11,045 feet high above the townsite. There were no trees anywhere, so there was no material for lumber, and consequently Ballarat was literally created out of clay. Its buildings were built of adobe bricks baked in the sun. Some residents added suitable ornaments and additions of corrugated iron, bottles, etc. Enough timbers were imported for lintels, doorframes and sills. In this barren, waterless waste there grew no little flower gardens, or yellow roses, as in other camps, only skimpy sagebrush and greasewood.

The town was actually a center for several mining camps, including the almost inaccessible Panamint City which hardly provided a level spot large enough for a dance floor. In Ballarat were found several dance places as well as the necessary adjuncts such as refreshments and ladies.

After the town died, it had a solitary inhabitant for years. This was "Shorty" Harris. In 1934 he died and Ballarat and he became ghosts together.

The adobe buildings are nearly melted away, but the remnants are well worth visiting, a monument to man's persistent search for gold in the face of almost insurmountable difficulties.

LONELY, WEATHERED REMNANT of business building strikes note of pathos against Panamints. Land is harsh, offering no timber, water, food. All supplies had to be hauled long distances. Yet Ballarat was scene of many gay times, even advertised a "Fancy Dress Ball."

In later years a tram was built from a huge terminal close to the mine down the precipitous mountainside, leaping from crag to crag and alighting at Keeler. On this web of steel rolled the ore buckets, eliminating the mule teams, since supplies came up easily in the emptied buckets, powered by the down-going ones. Machinery was needed, though not for power but to hold back and control the flow down the cliffs.

In 1959 the tram house and machinery were taken down, to be used in new mining operations near Candelaria, Nevada. Some towers and cables, complete with a bucket or two, have been left.

ANCIENT MULE COLLARS hang in groups on pegs in livery stable, now partly open to the sky.

"AMERICAN HOUSE" STANDS nearly 5,000 feet above now-dry Owens Lake. Sierra rises on other side. Hotel did not have private bath in every room, but even so, ran up monthly water bill of $300. Commodity had to be hauled up by mule teams from artesian well near Owens Lake. Guests were admonished to be "sparing with the water."

SWANSEA, CALIFORNIA

Here was a good-sized livery stable, the forge almost intact. There was a boardinghouse with wide porches, once screened. A well-worn path led to a hole in the ground, a vanished "convenience." White talc rocks lined both sides of the trail, whether to satisfy the aesthetic senses or to facilitate stumbling feet in the darkness would be hard to tell. Adjoining the kitchen was a chicken pen of wire. A short trip from the coop to the table!

The town was named Swansea after the famous smelter town in Wales. Mary Austin has given the whole area a fitting name—"The land of little rain."

There is a dry lake a few miles back of the edge of the steep cliff. Its bottom is pure salt, and it's called Saline Lake. The salt was hauled to the edge of the cliff; then run down on a tram cable to the terminus, where it was shipped across the lake to Cartago, from there to San Pedro, thence to Swansea, Wales for refining.

BOARDINGHOUSE STANDS on east shore of vanished Owens Lake (background). Above, to west looms loftiest section of high Sierra, whose once-copious snows nourished lake. Mt. Whitney is above chicken-run at right.

MEMORIES GHASTLY & GHOSTLY

WHITE HILLS, ARIZONA

In a truly desert setting, five miles from the highway, lie the scattered remnants of one of the wildest camps in Arizona.

This was White Hills, so named for the backdrop of blazingly white, rocky ridges. The buildings are few and lean toward each other, as if seeking support in their senility.

There is little rubbish in White Hills. The dooryards seem to have been swept recently; the glaring sand is smooth and neat. Many Joshua trees and bisnagas, the barrel cacti, have grown up to form landscaping.

CEMETERY IS OVER-GROWN by "Bisnagas," barrel cacti. These are of type reputed to have saved many desert travelers from death by thirst. If the top is chopped off, the interior pulp mashed into a hollow, copious juice collects and is perfectly p o t a b l e, if somewhat insipid.

"FRONT YARD" OF miner's cottage in White Hills is paved with dazzling white gravel, landscaped with typical desert plants, cacti and gnarled Joshua trees.

The place was not so tidy in the 1890's. There were 1,900 rough-and-ready miners then, not to mention their unsavory hangers-on. Water was brought in from distant mountain springs, but who drank it? Not many, judging from the piles of whiskey bottles on the fringes.

Rats were a serious problem in the town, living sumptuously on the garbage left everywhere. Cats were imported, to become a problem in turn when they multiplied apace, as cats will do. These then became targets for gun practice, their neglected bodies adding to the general stench.

The town suffered a number of cloudbursts, furnishing an embarrassingly large amount of water all at once, to the point of washing outhouses into the open desert.

Wandering around the immediate vicinity reveals innumerable mine headings, shafts and tunnels centered by the mill ruins.

CHLORIDE, ARIZONA

Here is a town whose classification is dubious because it has changed its status from living to dead and back again several times. Right now it is in-between, with plenty of the old for interest and with a certain amount of respiration not too noticeable.

In this last category is the little, newish building not more sizable than many a living room. It fronts on the main street and bears the proud sign "Chloride City Library." The movie house, on the other hand, shows a view of sagebrush and cacti through the boxoffice. And so it goes with Chloride. One of its ups was a good turquoise mine, owned by Tiffany of New York. One of its downs was the calamity, common to all silver towns, of the collapse in silver values.

Just when a big silver boom had pumped the veins of Chloride full of blood, the deflation period set in. This began in 1884, and when it ended by the demonitization of silver in 1893, Chloride's collapse was complete, at least as of then.

RELIC OF LATER BOOM was movie house. Through once ornate entrance one now sees a framed view of sagebrush and abandoned shacks.

GOLDROAD, ARIZONA

Sensible people, and those in a hurry to get from here to there, take the newer U. S. highway 66 from Kingman to Needles. But Ghost Town hunters branch off to the right five miles from Kingman. After a stretch of interesting, flattish desert the old road climbs breathtakingly toward Sitgreaves Pass, 3,500 feet above sea level.

Almost directly, upon starting down the other side, appear traces of buildings, the outskirts of Goldroad. Trickling downward to an only slightly wider stretch of canyon, the small stream of remnants spreads out a little into the main part of what was once an impressive mining camp.

At the close of a bonanza period of prosperity, with the price of gold making all further operations unprofitable, the buildings were sacrificed to avoid taxes. Since many structures were of adobe and stone because of limited supplies of timber, these unburnable ones leave fairly substantial ruins.

Vegetation surrounding them is of the sparsest, but is most interesting. There are many Ocotillos, Chollas and others, all full of thorns. The cliffs form walls all around and even a casual survey reveals mine shafts, heads, mills and dumps dotting the steepest walls, some clinging precariously after the fashion of those in the San Juan Mountains of Colorado.

EVEN THICKEST STONE WALLS crumble under onslaught of years. Pathetic remains were once home to miner's family, now offer scant shade to Gila monsters, rattlesnakes, rodents. Canyon in background holds main town and mines. Distant mountain range extends to Colorado River.

OLEANDER, PAMPERED HOTHOUSE SHRUB of most of country, survives years of neglect beside old miner's cabin in Goldroad. "Retaining wall" was built of old cyanide cans filled with ore. Mine dumps are seen in right background, road snakes down rocky ramparts.

ONE OF MOST IMPOSING structures in "downtown Goldroad" was made of sun-dried mud and chopped weeds, "adobe" style but not usual bricks. Material was apparently poured in forms as in concrete construction. Walls, foundations and buildings can be seen scattered in background.

OATMAN, ARIZONA

Oatman was named for a family which had camped near Gila Bend in 1851. It consisted of the mother and father, two daughters and a son. The Oatmans were attacked by a marauding band of Apaches, the parents killed, the boy, Lorenzo, beaten to unconsciousness and the girls kidnapped. When a detail of soldiers was sent out to effect their rescue, the sisters, Olive and Mary Ann were hidden by their captors at a small spring a half mile north of town and then spirited away. Mary Ann died later, but Olive was released in 1856 and joined her brother at Fort Yuma. She married John Fairchild in New York State in 1865 and died in Texas in 1903.

In its earlier days Oatman boasted a narrow gauge railway. It ran from the mines to Fort Mojave on the Colorado, to which point supplies were ferried from Needles, California.

During this period of ascendancy, Oatman took $3,000,000 in gold from its sterile, craggy site and boasted two banks, ten stores and a Chamber of Commerce.

"MOST FAMOUS SALOON IN ARIZONA" is proud boast of few remaining residents. Structure was known as "Mission Inn," upper floor once rested on ground, was raised and new section built beneath. Some differences of opinion exist as to purpose of many cubicles, each with one of numbers 1 to 18, upstairs. Some say they were "offices," others "gambling joints" or "apartments." Quartzite obelisk "Elephant's Tooth" looms in background.

NELSON, NEVADA

Nelson had once been called Eldorado, a name full of Spanish romance and suggestive of riches beyond counting, and indeed Spaniards had made the original discoveries of gold in this spot which now bears the name, Eldorado Canyon.

That was in 1775, but nothing much happened for a hundred years, when things got going under gringo ownership. The main operation became the notorious Techatticup Mine; notorious because wanton killings became so frequent there as to be almost commonplace. These were the results of disagreements over ownership, management or labor disputes, and the canyon with the romantic beginning became as sinister as the black rocks forming its walls.

Even so, the mine and its satellites produced several millions in gold, silver, copper and lead, before lowered values caused general cessation. The row of huge cyanide vats still form an imposing ruin.

HUGE VATS USED FOR PROCESSING GOLD ORE by cyanide treatment stand rotting in blistering heat of Eldorado Canyon. Vats are near cave where Indian "Public Enemy No. 1" named Quejo was discovered dead after 10 years of terrorizing area. His excuse for his crimes always was that he had been ordered by authorities to track down and slay his killer brother and to bring back the head as proof.

GOODSPRINGS, NEVADA

"Things are quiet here," Sam McClanahan said, "if people keep on moving away this ain't going to be nothing but a damned Ghost Town."

He had seen the early boom days when Goodsprings was a lusty young camp producing not only gold but a wealth of other minerals, silver, platinum and vanadium.

These are still to be found and, if their recovery could be accomplished cheaply enough, would pay off. But the old mill, an extensive one, is a collapsed mass of ruined ovens, walls and machinery. Sam told the same old story of frozen gold prices, advanced labor and machinery costs. Fondling his ancient gold pan he surmised that "some day, we'll get going again, when gold advances." He showed me some pieces of tufa, a light, foamy type of rock which he had found in the nearby hills. With capital, he said, he could build motels of this material which would provide insulation, "and those tourists in Las Vegas could come up here and get away from the heat."

But old Sam didn't really feel all this would come to pass. Like many other gnarled old-timers of the western Ghost Towns, he was just reluctant to admit that the town he had lived with so long will soon join the ranks of those decaying remnants of another day.

WEATHERED AND GNARLED, long-time resident of Goodsprings, Sam McClanahan holds beloved gold pan beside little garden plot, fenced against animals. Soil for vegetables was carried down from mountains. Water, a rarity in most of area, is here fairly abundant.

MINERS KEPT WARM on chilly Nevada nights in winter by pot-bellied stove, now rusting away outside door of tiny cabin.

REMAINS OF OLD MILL are extensive. During heyday, mining and ore refining operations employed several hundred men. Single ones spent most of time in bordellos at edge of town.

WHERE TIME STANDS STILL and there is no "progress," outdoor "conveniences" are still prominent feature. Even such lowly structure exhibits beautiful textures of weathered wood.

ONE OF EARLIEST RESIDENCES has remaining stone wall propped. Door opens only into more open s p a c e. Goodsprings is center of highly mineralized area, azurite, chrysocolla, malachite, cinnabar are among many prized specimens found on dumps of mines in past. Sources are nearly depleted now.

CALICO, CALIFORNIA

Calico is unique among ghost towns, a reconstructed and restored replica of the original. The man responsible for the feat should know what it looked like, for he worked there in the mines in 1910. He is Walter Knott, who now owns the whole town. The job has been no small project and is not finished yet.

The reason for the name is strikingly evident. The mountains forming a backdrop for the old camp are as brilliantly varied in color as any fabric could be.

Many of the buildings in Calico were made of adobe, sun-dried brick, for lack of sufficient lumber. These had partly melted away, even in this almost rainless country, and have been reconstructed of concrete, roughened and colored in such a way as to resemble closely the original appearance. Every now and then we would spot a frame building in its original condition. No amount of skill could duplicate the beautiful weathering effect only time and the elements can give to exposed wood.

The main street was not called "Main" but "Wall Street." In the 80's there were five saloons, three restaurants, many stores and hotels in addition to the usual boarding-houses, assay offices and school. Cornish miners (as in many early camps) were there in numbers and many of these lived in caves in the hills. These were secure from wind and were no doubt much cooler than the town's man-made structures. Daytime temperatures around the Calico Hills in summer will often reach 110 degrees or more.

Top producing days for Calico Mine were in the 80's. The number of saloons, always an indication of the size and prosperity of the population, was listed at more than twenty at this period.

The town began to die in 1892 and became more feeble until 1929, when it lay down and quit breathing entirely.

LITTLE SCHOOLHOUSE is lovingly rebuilt with original design in mind. Hill behind shows all the colors of calico cloth.

SKILLFUL BLENDING OF OLD with pseudo-old is evident here. Original signs seldom survive, but if these are re-creations they have authentic flavor.

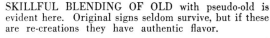

THEY REST IN PEACE

BODIE, CALIFORNIA

As early as August, 1865, Bodie attracted such nationwide attention by its wickedness and flagrant disregard of law and order that *Harper's Monthly* sent out a man to "case" the town for a story. He was I. Ross Browne. Having at last arrived there tired and dusty, he was encouraged to sit up and take notice by a slug of snake medicine. His eyes having thus been opened, he looked around him and found the place "destitute of vegetation" with the exception of sagebrush and grass. Mr. Browne missed a few details. There were also Argenomes, a prickly "poppy" and an iris.

For some Fourth of July celebrations trees and shrubs were imported for the day. These "Fourth of July" affairs were indeed important. The entire population turned out, many ladies were in formal gowns. As the day wore on lubrication progressed, and by the time the Grand Ball started in the evening things were really lively even if the imported verdure had wilted.

Dances were held in the Miners' Union Hall which still stands today. Many fights developed and combatants were ejected to continue the often fatal fracas outdoors. If a corpse resulted no one worried too much about it, but the next day a question had to be settled. On the hill close to town there were two burying grounds, one for the "decent respectable folks," the other, larger and more populous, for all the rest, so which one should properly hold the newcomer?

The "Bad Man from Bodie" is a well-founded legend. He is a compounded figure, made up of real-life rascals who infested the town. Among these were two Mexicans who had learned of the planned movement of $30,000 in bullion. They waylaid the coach on the stage road between Bodie and Carson City and got away with the loot. They were caught shortly but the gold was missing. One was killed in the capture, the other died in the Bodie jail overnight. Presumably the bandits cached the gold in the short time between hold-up and capture, but the secret of the location was buried with Pedro on Boot Hill. This was in 1880, but the gold is still there.

Maiden Lane and Virgin Alley were the two streets comprising the "red light" district. Houses ranged from mere cabins with one girl to the elegant high grade salon. Whereas loggers in the northern woods towns brought their girl friends pitchy wood for starting fires, the miners of Bodie filched nuggets of gold for theirs.

As much gold remains under Bodie Butte as was taken out, some $75,000,000 worth, but the vast labyrinth of tunnels and shafts under the Butte and town are collapsing into one another, and water fills the lower levels.

One day, when the price of gold advances, life may return to Bodie. But it is not likely to be the same violent, rowdy and lusty force which once animated the place and its 10,000 people.

The main street, named for *Harper's* Mr. Browne, once lined solidly with commercial buildings, has dwindled to a few blocks of sparsely spaced structures. Some of the most historic ones remain; the Firehouse with its old hose cart, Assay Office and Miners' Union Hall. On side streets are the Methodist Church, the jail, the school and a good many others.

SIDE STREET LEADS to Methodist Church. Funds for building quaint structure were solicited from redlight district, bordellos, saloons and opium dens as well as more legitimate business. The former contributed bulk of necessary funds. Metal roof added in later years has prevented total decay of charming little building.

HIGH SIERRA SHOWS over town. Central group of remaining business buildings is at right. Left of these and lower is old schoolhouse with many of its furnishings still intact. Motley collection of houses includes mostly homes. Freight and ore wagon is example of many weathering away in Bodie. Hand brake was often inadequate on steep mountain grades.

SHEEP NOW ROAM once busy streets. Ruins of stone buildings may be seen in background. Area is general location of once large Chinatown. Opium dens were openly operated on large scale, contributing to Bodie's unsavory reputation as the West's most wicked camp. Hundreds of Chinese population were buried outside of cemetery fence, which enclosed only those judged "respectable."

INTERIOR OF DESERTED home shows imported wall-paper flying in wind.

STUDY IN TEXTURES is old wood of wall and saw-horse.

DOORWAY OF BANKER CAIN'S home. James Stuart Cain was moving force in Bodie's big times, sustaining strength as it began to fail, never lost faith in its future. Starting in lumberyard in Carson City (supplying building supplies to Virginia City), Jim and new bride, Delilah, moved to Bodie in 1879. He bought into the Bodie railroad, then into the Standard Mine, which shortly after struck a ledge producing $90,000 in three months. Buying the Bodie Bank in 1890, he was on his way. Bank survived fire of 1892 only to perish in later general holocaust.

LARGEST GROUP OF business buildings faces morning sun. Scant survivors were once part of long street full of similar structures. In front of typically western style stores and saloons were held more-than-average number of holdups, shoot-outs and plain murders.

MASONIC, CALIFORNIA

The bones of Masonic lie bleaching in the sun, huddled in a canyon close to the Nevada border. The elevation is enough to allow a sparse forest of small nut pine trees to clothe the hills above the town, supporting a colony of squirrels.

The animals are the only inhabitants now where once nearly a thousand people cast their lot for a few short years of prosperity.

The town is divided into lower, middle and upper sections, the central one being the oldest and largest. Most of the remaining ruins are here. There are some houses in fairly good repair, but most are ready to collapse and are filled with vines and debris. Here stood an enormous mill, now in ruins. It had received its raw material via an extensive tram system from the mines some distance away. The cars still dangle from the cables, and look ready to move at any time.

Gold was first discovered here in the 1860's and the Jump Up Joe mine soon was operating at the site. "Middle Masonic" grew up around the mill which was built at a more accessible location than the mine itself, accounting for the tram.

After the greatest values were exhausted, about 1901, Warren Loose of Bodie bought the claim. Extensive cyanide operations for more efficient extraction employed some fifty men by 1904.

Operations grew steadily less and less after those big days and at last ceased entirely.

Masonic is not well known to anyone now except sheepherders, who sometimes drive a band of "woolies" through the town, temporarily giving an atmosphere of life and sound.

"MAIN STREET," Masonic, California, was busy thoroughfare at turn of century. Pinon pines sparsely cover hill above town, nuts are bonanza to rodents, now the only residents of once roistering camp.

MASONIC'S TINY POST OFFICE was located in "Middletown" section. Window at right of door slid aside for dispersal of mail to eager, homesick miners. Flimsy little flagpole still stands, wired to building.

UNIQUE COMBINATION houses "convenience," left, chicken house, right. Former was lined with carpet and cardboard to help keep out wintry blasts, was "one holer." Hen house was complete with roosts for six birds, hopefully had nesting boxes for four. Tiny chicken run is at right.

PINE GROVE, NEVADA

The best-preserved building in Pine Grove was apparently once a business headquarters, for a rusty safe lay just outside. A ruined picket fence surrounded the house, covered with withered hop vines. One of the vines still showed life, a forlorn sprig in the dead town. At one side of the door was a faded typewritten notice. "You are welcome to live here but please do not tear down."

Another building, the cookhouse, had several layers of paper on its walls, tattered and peeling off. The first layer was of newspapers, mainly the *San Francisco Chronicle* and *World Report*. These carried the dates from 1891 to 1897. Over this was fancy imported wallpaper. Later newpapers covered the torn elegance and the latest of these were dated in the early 30's.

The original discovery of gold in the area was in 1866. Within a year, Pine Grove had 300 people. There were three mills shipping $10,000 in gold bullion every week. The population continued to expand, then dwindled, grew again and, about the time the fancy wallpaper was added, in the 1880's, was at its height. The last small flurry occurred when the latest newspapers were pasted on the walls to keep out the cold winter winds. With the 1930's went the last inhabitants and Pine Grove has become a true Ghost.

DINING ROOM IN BOARDINGHOUSE seems ready to serve meal. However, accumulated dust of many years covers table and floor has two inches of dried, cracked mud.

IMPRESSIVE STONE RUINS of once busy general store. Occupying central position in original location of Pinegrove, it suffered by later removal of business section half a mile up c a n y o n where boardinghouse and school remain. Portal now stands alone, looking out on hills scarred and torn by mine operations.

PINEGROVE SCHOOL is within 200 feet of stamp mill. Pinegrove permitted little "rough stuff" because of sizable proportion of children. S i n g l e miners went to nearby Rockland for "h e l l raising," there being several saloons and bawdy houses there.

PHANTOMS OF THE FAR WEST

JACKSONVILLE, OREGON

Original discoveries of gold were on Jackson Creek, in December, 1851. By the middle of the summer the place was already swarming with prospectors and miners of claims already staked out and the city of Jacksonville was on its way.

This frenzied activity was interrupted for a time when the Rogue River Indian wars of 1855 broke out, but resumed at the cessation of hostilities.

A smallpox epidemic in 1868, a flood in 1869 and fire upon fire ravaged the village, but never seriously discouraged the populace.

Advent of the Civil War split the people into factions, however, and did more to cause of dissension and strife than all the natural disasters put together. But that too, passed away and left the town in the peace it still enjoys today in a somnolent but living atmosphere.

Jacksonville is not a dead ghost, but neither is it a lively one, except for the tourists who visit this fascinating monument to Oregon's mining history.

CROWDED GRAVES ARE SUBMERGED in dense grove of cypress and madrona. These last are indigenous to area and are striking with peeling red trunks and evergreen leaves, clusters of orange-yellow berries.

FIRST PROTESTANT CHURCH west of the Rockies.
Covered wagon is "prop" of Oregon's centennial year.

WELL-FORTIFIED AGAINST bandits and Indians was
this building, dating from 1856.

PETER BRITT STANDS OUT among early-day photographers. His studio is set up in the museum located in the
old courthouse. Beautiful structure was built in 1883. Courtroom upstairs is preserved intact.

HOSKINS, OREGON

The remains of Hoskins nestle in a hollow at the edge of the Coast Range, just where the mountains merge with the level flood plain of the Willamette River.

Due to a concentration of Indians at Siletz Agency in 1856, Fort Hoskins was established on the Luckiamute River near the mouth of what is now Bonner Creek, on July 26th of that year. The Fort was named for Lt. Charles Hoskins who had been killed in the battle of Monterrey, Mexico, ten years before.

Lumber was king in those days and the timber to be sawed grew densely there. Virgin forests were so dense as to shut out the light of day except at noon. Sawmills sprang up all along the coast range.

As the woods were depleted close by, short logging railways were extended to the diminishing forests. About 1918 the Valley and Siletz Railroad laid tracks through Hoskins displacing the old store, a relic of the 1880's. The venerable building was moved to a new location a few hundred feet down the slope and beside the tracks.

Mr. Earl Lonie, who now owns the store, says, "But I guess they had some wild times upstairs in the old days." It is easy to imagine the ladies and gentlemen, perspiring from the performance of a lively two-step, walking out on the little balcony for a cooling breath of air.

A number of abandoned houses and cabins are scattered about, no pattern of streets exists any more for Hoskins, and as Mr. Lonie sadly remarked, "The place seems to be a thing of the past."

COVERED BRIDGE LEADS to Hoskins. Many of these structures may be found in back ways of area. Luxuriant foliage of maples and firs is in sharp contrast to stark bareness of towns of "Great Basin" recently visited.

ANTIQUE CABOOSE dates from 1870's. Crossed bars
on sides were for reinforcement. Probably even they
would not hold venerable car together now. Repair
shops with walls full of parts is in background.

OLD-TIME RAILROAD MAN, Robert Norris, says
"Bent rods with fastening loops in ends were used under
caboose and cars to prevent rigging and other operating
parts from falling to tracks should they come loose."

KERBY, OREGON

James Kerby (or Kerbey) spelled his name first one way, then the other, and confusion still hovers over the spelling, not only of his name, but that of the town named for him. The town seems to have first been called Kirbey's Ranch, then Kerbyville. Then for a time it was named Napoleon! In 1857, D. S. Holton got control of most of the town and decided, since it was in Josephine County, Napoleon would be an elegant and appropriate title. The name was popular only with him and the town soon reverted to plain Kerby.

Kerby was well established by 1850, and in 1858 took over the position of county seat. As usual, gold was the main attraction, but many other minerals have been mined in the area, including iron, quicksilver, cobalt and ilmenite. Infusoria earth and quartz have had their day, too.

At its best, Kerby had a population of 500 or more miners and the usual proportion of hangers-on.

About this time, a neighboring mining town contracted for an elegant pool table, to be packed in in sections on the backs of mules. The expedition started from Crescent City, California. On camping one night near Kerby, one mule with the most important part of the table turned up missing. When found in the morning, he was dead. The packer decided he had gone far enough, buried his mule and established his pool hall in Kerby.

The town populace has dwindled to a mere handful, but a typical group of buildings remains, including the Masonic Temple, a tiny store, and several false fronts.

Across the street is a huge oak which is supposed to have been the inevitable "Hanging Tree," for the only ghost town without a "Hanging Tree" is a town with no trees at all. In this case, since the old Courthouse stood in its shade, and convicted prisoners were dragged out and hanged immediately, the tree certainly would have been convenient for this grisly use.

"HANGING TREE" broods over remnant of Kerby.

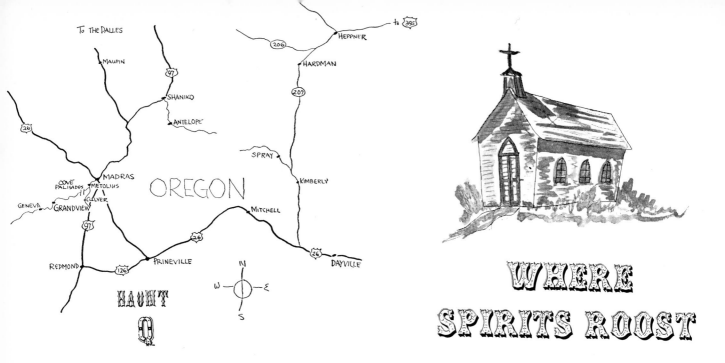

HARDMAN, OREGON

In the days of stagecoaches two small Oregon towns were bitter rivals for the stage depot in their area. They were Raw Dog and Yellow Dog, about a mile apart in Morrow County, Oregon.

In the 1870's many stagecoaches and wagon trains traveling north and south through eastern Oregon and Washington, found one or the other of the two towns a convenient overnight resting place. This business was much more lucrative and easy than the regular ranching and cattle operation. Passengers found themselves shunted from one place to the other as drivers were favored or even bribed to stay the night.

Then, late in the decade, the rivalry became even more intense because it became known that a post office would be established in the area.

The whole thing was settled when Raw Dog was found to have several more people than Yellow Dog and was declared to be the metropolis and a fitting location for a United States Post Office. This move also decided the location of a more permanent stagecoach station and the demise of Yellow Dog was complete. Its remaining inhabitants moved over to the town that "had everything"' and their abandoned stores and buildings, such as they were, completely disappeared.

Now, as a veritable kennel of "dog towns," Raw Dog became just that . . . Dog Town and was so known for many years. When the post office was officially established in 1881, however, the dignitaries frowned on the name Dog Town and instead called the newborn

GENERAL VIEW OF TOWN from cemetery on hill above town. Clouds sweep in from south, but promise of rain is false in summer, usually dry. Two painted buildings are permanently occupied, others temporarily or not at all.

post office Hardman, after the man who had homesteaded the site. So Hardman it was officially known, but the dog tag hung on it for many years.

The town flourished and grew. A large hotel was built just south of the Odd Fellows Hall, and smaller hostelries sprang up along the main street.

There was even a jail, built of 2 x 6 inch lumber laid flat, and considered impregnable. One morning after a particularly boisterous Halloween, however, it was found tipped over on its side. It stayed that way until the following Halloween, when it was set afire, and "made a very hot blaze" according to an old resident.

Parker's Sawmill was located about 15 miles southeast near the pine woods, and contributed much to the economy. More important to the more lively element was the big all-day celebration and dance held every Fourth of July. These annual events were not always conducted with as much decorum as they might have been.

A large flour mill did a good business grinding the local wheat. It stood at the extreme south end of town. A drugstore with the typical false front of its day was built just north of the present grocery store. In front, in the middle of a wooden platform extended from the board sidewalk, was a handpump for water. Since there was no central water system and many people had no well, the pump was a community affair, and news of the townspeople spread rapidly from there.

With the decline of the stagecoaches and wagon trains, and as travel speeded up, the main usefulness of Hardman began to fade away and the town pump served fewer and fewer people. The community slid into a decline from which it will never recover.

HARDMAN MARKS southern edge of wheatfields. Drugstore in background once stood on Main Street.

SHANIKO, OREGON

"Shaniko is the wool center of the world" proudly boasted its citizens of an earlier day. Cornered, they might admit, "Well, if not of the world, at least of the Pacific Northwest." And this came very near the truth.

Shaniko owed its birth to wool, and to wheat. No accidental gold strike or gradual accretion of farmers produced the town. Shaniko's was a planned birth.

Central Oregon, in the 1890's was, in effect, one huge sheep ranch. Wool was produced in enormous quantities and the only outlet for these thousands of bales of fleece was The Dalles, Oregon. Then in 1898, in order to expedite the shipment of wool from the countless bands of sheep which extended to Lakeview and the California line, a railroad was constructed from Biggs Junction, on the Columbia River.

Since a railroad couldn't be useful without some kind of terminal, Shaniko was built for that express purpose. It was the brainchild of a group of bankers and businessmen in The Dalles and Moro and was first laid out as a tent town, but by 1900 many permanent buildings were put up, including the hotel, a combination City Hall, Fire Hall and jail, and a general store, all of which still stand. In rapid succession followed many other structures. Many of these have succumbed to time, fire and vandals. A school was built with funds raised by popular subscription.

Actually, Shaniko was preceded by another settlement, or rather a small community, gathered around a stagecoach station called Cross Hollows, because of the two gullies

OLD SCHOOL WAS BUILT in 1902 with funds raised by "passing the hat" according to Frank Wagner who lived there 43 years. Any school children now must make trip to Maupin schools.

HOTEL WAS BUILT AT turn of century, still serves excellent home-cooked meals at long table, "family style." Tall "City Hall" across street had council chambers upstairs. Fire hose-cart and jail cells occupy ground floor. Structure is surrounded by empty spaces once filled by business buildings.

PRESENT POST OFFICE was established in this building about 1906. Structure in background was drugstore, smaller one leaning against it was pool hall. Rotting wooden sidewalks extend many empty blocks beyond in sagebrush.

having their intersection there. The spot was a natural stopping place for stagecoaches on their way from The Dalles and other points. The station was owned and operated by John and Elizabeth Ward. In 1874, a German immigrant named August Scherneckau arrived and bought out the Wards. Being industrious and possessed of many other good qualities, he prospered. A post office was established for the expanding village on May 23, 1879 with the benevolent and bearded head man as first postmaster.

By 1887, Mr. Scherneckau was well off financially and decided to retire, and spend the rest of his days in California. All the Indians in that part of central Oregon were fond of him and regretted his going, although none of them could correctly pronounce his Germanic name. And so they called the place Shaniko. Having sold out to one Gustav Schmidt, Scherneckau departed to Astoria to catch a ship south. But the city of Astoria so appealed to him that he stayed there until 1923, when he decided to take a long deferred trip to California. This he did, but his stay was short. He died in 1925 and was returned to Astoria, where he is buried.

The site for Shaniko had been chosen for the same reason the original station was built there. A good reliable water supply existed on the spot.

The Cross Hollows post office ceased to exist in 1887 with the departure of its Postmaster. With the establishment of Shaniko Post Office on March 31, 1900, with John D. Wilcox as postmaster, the era of the original Cross Hollows settlement was officially ended.

Shaniko now is only a faint shadow of its former self. Wooden sidewalks run out to nothing and are bordered only by grass and weeds.

ANTELOPE, OREGON

The gay 90's were not only gay in Antelope, but punctuated by shootings and brawls in the best western town tradition. And in common with so many tinder-dry and nearly waterless towns, it suffered trial by fire in 1898 and was nearly wiped out.

Antelope is situated in a small valley of the same name, so called first by someone in the party of Joseph H. Shearer, who was engaged in packing supplies to the John Day mines in 1862.

The road to Antelope consisted of two ruts through the sagebrush in the 60's and for a long time thereafter. Stagecoaches bumping along over rough terrain ran more smoothly when they entered the little valley where so many antelope fed and watered. Passengers were glad to stop and eat or stay overnight at the stage station, newly erected. This entailed a little hotel and a blacksmith shop. Also, inevitably, came a saloon. This was owned and operated by F. W. Silvertooth, who had driven a stage from The Dalles to Canyon City and decided to settle here.

By the year 1871, the place expanded to the point where a post office became possible, and on the seventh of August it was opened.

A prime figure in the history of Central Oregon was appointed first postmaster, intrepid Howard Maupin, who left his print on so many places in the state. It was he who, tiring of having stock stolen by Chief Paulina, tracked that wily Indian down and killed him near Paulina Basin, putting an end to depredations that had harassed the pioneers in the valley for years.

The town grew apace, being a natural center for cattlemen and later sheepmen. It was a convenient stopping place for supply wagons and enjoyed prosperity for a few years. More saloons went up. One of these was run by partners named Benjamin Pratt and Ed Gleason. All was not harmony between them, however, as rumors were rife that Mr. Pratt fancied the wife of his partner. One fine morning in '85, as Pratt was unlocking the door of their business establishment, Mr. Gleason, a believer in gossip, walked up and shot his partner dead with a rifle.

The trial was a cursory Kangaroo Court sort of affair. It was decided that the outraged husband was justified in eliminating Mr. Pratt from the scene.

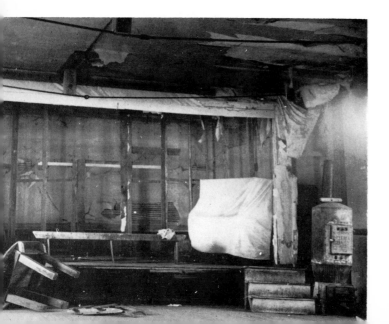

TINY STAGE AT END OF dance hall once looked on gay balls, Christmas parties, lodge gatherings and just plain dances.

SUPERIMPOSED SIGNS TELL varied occupancy over years. Starting out as carriage and blacksmith shop it served later as furniture store. At beginning of a u t o era, venerable building converted to garage for short time before dying completely.

R. J. Pilkington was Antelope's first doctor, serving the town all through the 90's. In addition to his practice, Dr. Pilkington operated a drugstore in the old saloon building.

The disastrous fire of '98 started in Tom Condon's Bowling Alley, above which were his family living quarters. After he had seen the women safely down, Condon's escape was cut off by flames. Outside the window was the pulley and rope by which water was raised to the apartment. Fortunately the bucket was at the top and ready. The resourceful Condon straddled the bucket and let himself down the rope. The town itself was not so lucky. After the holocaust, only one of the original buildings on the main street was left standing, as it still does today, at the far end of the street.

The town was rebuilt almost immediately, and things went pretty much as before. The little main street with its one surviving structure was solidly lined again, but this newer phase of the town's history was to end also. The town of Shaniko had been born only eight miles north as terminus of a railroad from the Columbia River. The new town drained off the population of Antelope and eventually left it an empty shell.

LITTLE CHURCH SERVED Antelope for many years. Now idle, its doors stand open and town's few children romp up and down aisle. Tiny filigreed organ waits near pulpit, is in working order, birds nest in walls, their nesting holes can be seen in clapboards.

THE SILVERTOOTH ESTABLISHMENT also boasts a barbershop with business being conducted among relics of mining, cattle. Extensive rock collection completes resemblance of room to museum. Area is famous as source of agate of fancy quality, once abundant in huge chunks as "nuisances" in plowed fields. Gem stones are now much harder to find.

THE JAIL HOUSE, standing west of the dance hall was convenient place to hold rowdies.

JAIL ITSELF WAS FRAIL, but "cell block" within was stout, and safely held most belligerent drunks, one of whom set fire to his thin straw mattress, hoping to escape in resultant confusion. However, fire hose was inserted through little window, drenching mattress *and* occupant, suddenly subduing the latter, completing the sobering-up process.

EAST SIDE OF MAIN Street in Antelope has true atmosphere of w e s t e r n cattle town. The porch of the Silvertooth "Emporium" is banked by piles of agate and jasper.

TWO-STORY DANCE HALL had outside stairway and "conveniences." Tiny building at corner served as telephone office. Store and filling station no longer function. Tiny, new structure farther up street combines services for small remaining population and ranchers of area.

GRANDVIEW, OREGON

The road to Grandview descends into a deep, precipitous canyon, crosses two turbulent streams, and climbs out again to a typical, high plateau of central Oregon.

The snow peaks looking down on the site are even more spectacular and include a half dozen of the tallest in Oregon. The name "Grandview" does not exaggerate.

But there was exaggeration in the promises to the farmers and homesteaders who settled the place. There would be "plenty of water," "the land is good." They settled to work and found that the sharp rocks on the land were more than enough to make high stone fences all around the fields. The rocks were endless and dulled farm machinery.

Schools were built, homes, barns and a store which served also as a mail distributing center. The letters were hauled across the canyon from Madras.

Optimism was boundless. The settlement extended several miles toward the south and a second school was erected in the Geneva district.

But there was not enough water for this arid place. The junipers encroached upon the farms, the stones continually came to the surface. By the time the tiny cemetery held a dozen graves the town was being deserted, and by 1932 only a handful of people remained, their children going all the way to Culver to school.

Grandview is empty now, the schoolhouse filled with sheep hides, the fields covered with juniper trees and sagebrush.

LITTLE SCHOOLHOUSE served as church on Sundays, now stands deserted. Rusting farm machinery in schoolyard shows defeat in face of rocks, sagebrush and drought.

LARGE JUNIPER TREE shades dooryard of combination store and mail-station. Mail was hauled across canyon from Madras, distributed from here. Junipers and sagebrush are natural "flora" of area, jack rabbits, coyotes and ground squirrels the "fauna."

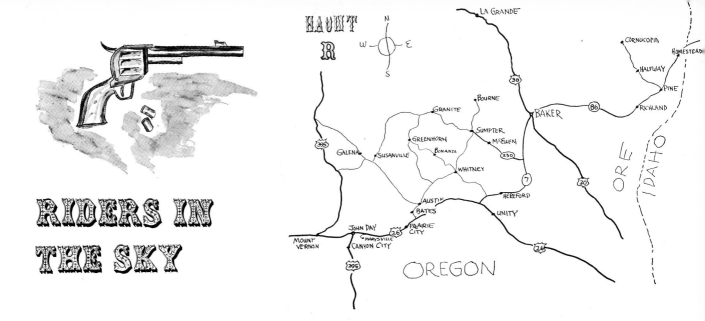

CORNUCOPIA, OREGON

Cornucopia was once a rip-roaring gold mining camp with over a thousand people. It boomed not once but several times, as each new lode of fabulously rich gold ore was followed up. Some of the ore was so full of free gold that nuggets could be shaken out of it. Eight saloons provided refreshment and entertainment to hundreds of rough miners, many of them from Cornwall, England and called, for some obscure reason, "Cousin Jacks."

The first big boom years were from 1884 to 1886. The Union Companion Mine was the big one then, but several others ranged on up the rugged slopes, the Last Chance being at 7,000 feet. As for the name of the town, Cornucopia, with its connotation of wealth and abundance, has always been a popular name for mining towns. Some of the early miners here had come from Cornucopia, Nevada, and named the new camp for the old.

Erma Cole was a child of eight when she arrived with her father and mother in Cornucopia. Her father had been mining in the Yellow Jacket near what is now Sun Valley, Idaho, but had been told to quit the mines as he suffered "miner's consumption." The little family traveled on horseback to Weiser, then to Red Bluff, California. Here Mr. Cole heard that a Mr. Shipman, who had been the bookkeeper of the Yellow Jacket, was now in charge at the mines at Cornucopia. Not having found work elsewhere, he decided to cast his lot in the mines again. The family set out in horse and buggy for Cornucopia, a long and arduous trip in those days.

When they arrived there in October, 1898, Cornucopia had already shed its first site and moved farther up the slope to be nearer the mines, although the school, several saloons and office of the only physician, Dr. O'Conner, remained on the old townsite.

The little girl and her mother sat in their buggy on Main Street for half an hour. "When father returned," Erma remembers, "he told us that he had a job at top wages; $3.50 a day. He had already rented a tiny house and bought a stove so we would be warm." Mother Cole was not happy; Joseph ought not work in the mines again, but there was no choice. The family was destitute. And sure enough, "Father lasted just 15 days and came down terribly ill with pneumonia." The Irish physician, Dr. O'Conner, was summoned from the lower town and reassured the frightened family by telling them he had never yet lost a pneumonia patient. Joseph Cole did get well, but could not return to the mine.

159

At this time the one street was lined on both sides for several blocks by the typical false fronts and many cabins. There was a livery stable across from the post office. The meat market boasted two floors, the residence of the proprietor being over the shop. Mr. Estes was the butcher, a huge man with very short legs. He went everywhere on his mule named Becky, pulling himself up into the saddle by sheer strength. A good-sized general store was on the west side of the street, owned by Tom Turner in those early days. Later he took in a partner named Brown.

One of the buildings was a hotel and, at that critical period in the fortunes of the Coles, it needed a cook and manager. "Mother was a wonderful cook and Father was able by now to take over the duties of clerk and manager. Together they made a go of it and for a time it seemed as though this would be permanent. The hotel was always full, as living quarters were scarce and Mother's cooking attracted business."

Winter snows were and are of a prodigious depth in that section of the Wallowa Mountains. Total depth in winter often reached 30 feet, or a settled depth of 10 feet. The two stages which came daily, one from Baker and the other from Union, used sled runners instead of wheels. All winter the little street lay buried deeply and the trail rose higher and higher, much above the level of the doorways.

"Father cut a tunnel from the door up to the trail, and carefully made beautiful steps in the hard-packed snow. As soon as he turned his back we kids used them for a delightfully bumpy ride on our sleds and it soon took the sharp edges off the steps and Father would have to make them all over again. Little brother, Robert, who was five, would never come down stairs the conventional way, but jumped out of his upstairs window onto the snow, often with all too few clothes on his small body. This particular winter he became ill with rheumatic fever and mother had to devote her full time to nursing the boy.

BARBERSHOP AND "CANDY STORE" are among buildings on Main Street of Cornucopia. Barbershop was post office before tonsorial conversion. Space between buildings was boarded up during winters and soon filled up with snow. It packed and was handy during summer for making ice cream treats.

EARLY-DAY BARN of logs still stands. Shake roof was steeply pitched to shed enormous winter snows. Even so, snow piled up and had to be removed by hand.

The cooking had to be turned over to hired help, an unsatisfactory arrangement which resulted in the sale of the hotel to George Herbert, who later was sheriff of Baker County."

At this time the mines were using huge amounts of timber for shoring up the tunnels and shafts, for sluice trestles and many other purposes. Although the town was surrounded by an immense stand of virgin timber, wood and timbers were in short supply for lack of cutters. So Mr. Cole turned to this occupation and it proved to be successful.

Things became easier for the Coles and another strike helped produce a new boom for the town. Had the rich streaks of gold been mined systematically the situation would have been more stable, but some companies gutted them, and miners had to be searched on leaving to go home at night. Their pockets and lunch boxes would sometimes be found to have golden linings.

Mine accidents were frequent. Men were blown to bits by premature blasts, tunnel walls caved in or were flooded. Fire took its toll and avalanches were frequent. Huge slides of snow sometimes buried buildings entirely, entombing luckless inhabitants.

An explosion made fatherless one of the playmates of the Cole children. He was Christopher Schneider, and at 12, he had to get a job to support his mother and sisters. He was industrious and well liked and soon was doing the important work of sharpening drills.

Erma and other camp children usually played near where Chris was working. They ranged the mine tunnels and, since there was little room left when the ore-filled cars came rolling along, they flattened themselves against the walls whenever this happened. Shafts hundreds of feet deep connected to the tunnels, but strangely, no child ever fell down one of them.

EARLY-DAY CONSTRUCTION shows interesting wood textures. This is corner of huge barn which sheltered large part of important population of mules and horses, used mostly in hauling of firewood, shoring and stope timbers for mines.

FORGOTTEN WAG nailed shoes to weathered pump house.

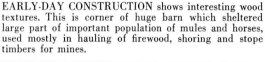

Cornucopia lacked the wild shooting frays and killings so characteristic of other mining towns in early days, but in common with them, had the usual quota of women who lived in a couple of buildings by themselves. Miss Cole delicately refers to these as "Sporting Ladies."

The madam of one of these was familiarly known as Fanny, and she took her meals at the hotel where the Coles stayed. Around the corner from the dining room was a closet in which was a barrel. The hotel's official mouser, a big white cat named "Snowball," had selected this as a nursery for her new litter of kittens. Came dinner time and Fanny swept in with one of her girls named Nelly. They were followed by her several dogs whose custom it was to wait attentively on the chance of a bone. But now the dogs were irresistibly attracted to the barrel. When Snowball exploded in their faces, the resulting confusion in the dining room was such that both Fanny and Nelly jumped up on the table and held their voluminous skirts well up out of the way. To quote Erma Cole again, "I was somewhat bold in those days and I couldn't help laughing at them, but they were very upset."

As Erma grew up she also worked, usually helping wait table for the single men, in the company mess hall. "It was all I could do to carry those enormous platters heaped high with steaks, and the tureens of soup, each with a big ladle. The men helped themselves and ate like beasts. They piled up outside the door, and at the signal, fell over each other in their haste to get into the dining hall. And, while they looked at us girls, it would have been as much as his life was worth for one of them to so much as touch us. The company saw to that."

Now Cornucopia is slowly reverting to wilderness, sagging and empty buildings sparsely line the main street. Trees grow up through collapsing porches and cedar shakes rattle in the winds, playing a wild tattoo on steeply pitched roofs. Pack rats frolic where miners and gay ladies danced on rough plank floors, and where games of "21" lasted all winter.

TRESTLE LED DOWN FROM mill and carried pipe line to pump house. Tailings in soupy sludge dropped by gravity and then were lifted to top of huge pile by pumps. House was near to being engulfed by its own dumpings when town died.

ORE CAR STANDS WHERE it was left at mouth of Coulter Tunnel. Mines, whose upper workings were many hundreds of feet higher on mountain, dropped their shafts to level of tunnel which was well lighted in later years and had a restaurant for miners carved out of solid granite and gold ore a mile and a quarter back in the mountain. Blast of icy air emerges from mouth.

GRANITE, OREGON

When the original prospectors and settlers arrived at Granite in 1862, they realized the date was July 4th and accordingly named the future town Independence. But the postal authorities said no, there already was an "Independence" in Oregon. Further consultation produced "Granite," for the prevailing rock of the region.

Until about twenty years ago the general store had a good supply of derby hats, black corsets with beaded tops, heavy "snuggy" underwear and brilliantly spangled women's garters.

Now the faded buildings stand empty and deserted, their ranks thinning by fire and collapse under winter snows.

IN FRONT OF OLD CEMETERY stands tiny schoolhouse. Later it served as polling place, a sort of "city hall." Pine-covered hill in background is typical of Blue Mountains. Seen from a distance through haze, heavy stands of ponderosa pines take on bluish look. Ancient headboards totter over forgotten graves behind plank fence at right.

NICKELODEON FACES drugstore across street. Until rather recent years structure also served as store and filling station. Grass-grown streets attest to lack of traffic now. Road carries cars to going mine in mountains and small private claims.

BOURNE, OREGON

Cracker was an honest, genuine gold mining and placering town in the 1870's and it had all the earmarks of the typical camp. A "Maiden Lane" section adjoined the several saloons and gambling houses; a large general store and hotel helped line the steeply inclined street. The main street was the only one, because the canyon sides all but squeezed out even that. At the upper end, however, there were several short, interesting "pieces" of streets perched here and there on the ledges. Each had its quota of businesses and residences in the days of Bourne's golden prosperity.

At the turn of the century Cracker began to deviate from honest mining and began to speculate. Somehow this more or less coincided with the change of name, although the new title honored a respected U.S. Senator, Jonathon Bourne. The Post Office of Bourne was established in March, 1895.

As Bourne, the place became a hotbed of inflationary get-rich-quick bubbles, all of which burst in short order.

Two newspapers emerged each week from the same printshop. One contained legitimate news. The other, meant for the outside world, promoted the myth that the town of Bourne was only a thin skin over a lode equal to the world's greatest bonanzas.

The closure of the post office in May, 1927, indicated the approaching end of this era and ten years later a cloudburst sent a wall of water down Cracker Creek and Main Street marking the finish of Bourne.

Enough remains to make a visit well worth while. Bourne is only about seven miles from Sumpter over a road typical of the more remote sections of the Blue Mountains, not good, not bad, not as steep as many, and lined with mementos of the boisterous days of gold placering along Cracker Creek.

UPPER END OF MAIN STREET of Bourne. Extensive foundations of large buildings are in background. Traces of all periods of former activity are scattered through town.

HYDRAULICKING GOES ON in small way along Cracker Creek below Bourne. Gold recovery still pays if not too much cost is involved. Here powerful head of water from small dam upstream is directed at gold-bearing mud and gravel; resulting thick liquid is channeled into sluice to settle out gold.

MARYSVILLE, OREGON

Nostalgia must have soon taken over the little group of prospectors from California. They had discovered traces of gold in Dog Creek near John Day, traced them to a good ledge on the hill and there founded a little town. This was in April of 1862, and they christened the infant camp Marysville after their home town.

In two years the place already had a population of several hundred and the juvenile element needed, though likely did not desire, a school. With contributions and a poll-tax one was built, this being the second school district in Grant County. It started off with twenty-one pupils and one teacher. This brave soul was a girl named Elizabeth Chope. The community spent $97.34 that first year.

The town was started so early, the buildings were so impermanent and have been abandoned so long that tracing its plan is difficult. Almost all of Marysville has melted away, leaving only the collapsed shell of the schoolhouse. Before long this, too, will have vanished.

PATHETIC REMAINS of little school crown bluff above canyon of John Day River. Rimrock scene is typical of eastern Oregon where low elevation and rainfall do not permit stand of timber.

SUMPTER, OREGON

The railroad came to Sumpter in 1896 because of the new veins of ore being opened and developed . . . or maybe it was the other way around. In any event, the population zoomed to 3,000 in no time. This was a big increase from the few hundred pioneer-type individuals who had patiently panned in the Powder River, and pecked away at the hard rock streaks of gold in the previous 20 years.

In 1862 three men from North Carolina built a log cabin on the site. They intended to farm the land, an ambition later swamped by the tide of gold mining.

They found a spherical rock almost like a cannonball nearby and were inspired by this discovery, along with severe nostalgia, to call their new home "Fort Sumter," a name prominent in those Civil War days.

The "Fort" was lost, but the "Sumter" remained, picking up a "P" somewhere along the way. Spelling in those days was regarded lightly.

For a good many years Sumpter flourished, feeding on new lodes opened by improved methods and the substantial returns from the huge dredges in the river. As these sources died out, so did Sumpter. Several disastrous fires took heavy toll as evidenced by parts of brick walls and exposed bank vaults.

Dredging operations have continued until the whole valley is in ruins, tailings occupying the creek bed and both banks. But since 1916 the town has declined. A few newer buildings are scattered among the ruins, and Sumpter would have had a chance to become a farming community, but for the preponderance of granite tailings over good soil.

VAULT IS ALL THAT remains of old bank, burned years ago in Sumpter. White Masonic Hall is on hill in background, was one of few wooden structures spared in holocaust.

AUSTIN, OREGON

Austin was not itself a mining camp, but a supply depot for the many busy gold towns in the Blue Mountain area. The little narrow gauge railroad from Sumpter had its terminus here for many years in the earliest days, later being extended to Prairie City.

During this bustling period Austin was supposed by everyone to have a brilliant, permanent future. There were three large sawmills going full blast, turning out lumber for Greenhorn, Bonanza and other flourishing towns higher up in the densely forested mountains. A substantial jail was necessary for the many rowdies, drunks and more serious offenders. Several stores and office buildings for doctors, lawyers and real estate operators were built.

Already long established was the hotel and stagecoach way-station started by Mr. Newton. It was later bought by Mr. and Mrs. Minot Austin and called the "Austin House," giving the now growing community its name. The post office was incorporated in the building in 1888. The station was still being used as a hotel for hunters as late as W.P.A. days.

The decline of the gold camps spelled the death of Austin which had depended upon their existence. The population which had totaled about 500 at its height dwindled to 50 at the close of the second World War and is at the vanishing point now.

AUSTIN HOUSE LOOKS BETTER now than in photo of 1900. Wing extending south is long gone. Square structure on adjoining section shows at left. Original loghouse stands to right, out of range of camera.

LOAD AND PASSENGERS seem mostly to be on outside of stage in picture taken 60 years before our record. Picture was kindly loaned us by present tenants, the Alton E. Roods.

CENTER OF CITY GOVERNMENT in Austin heyday was this gaunt building. Inside on main floor are two stout cells with heavy doors with strong iron hinges and hasps. Upstairs were offices of city fathers.

ANCIENT LOG STRUCTURE dates back to earliest days of gold discoveries in Blue Mountains. Standing near Austin House, it antedates that building, is now regarded as "just the woodshed."

GREENHORN, OREGON

The two young men fresh from the East were as ignorant as they could possibly be on mining lore. They were determined, however, to strike it rich with a gold mine. They had heard that almost anywhere "Out West" they could simply strike a pick in the ground and there would be gold in unlimited quantities. Why they picked on this tiny camp high in the Blue Mountains of Oregon no one knows. But they did, one day, about 1890, walk brashly up to the bar of the little saloon and ask the barkeep, "Where can we dig for gold in this place?"

After the man with the towel recovered his composure, he turned to some of the more seasoned customers and in turn inquired, "Well, where would *you* say these boys might hit a vein of gold?" One of the "regulars" seeing an opportunity for a joke, took them outside and at random pointed to the side of the hill above town, saying, "There's a likely looking spot to dig!"

And dig they dutifully did. In a moment they came back down to the now uproariously merry group lugging a chunk of rock, with the naive question, "How does this look?" Laughter died among the gathering. The piece of rock was "blossom" stuff, richer than anything yet discovered in the camp.

Ridicule vanished, the old-timers in all honesty directed the innocents to stake their claims immediately, but the mine's discoverers didn't get the chance to name their find. The wiseacres had already christened it, "The Greenhorn Mine." The camp changed *its* name to Greenhorn and as such burgeoned and grew into a real, full-scale town, complete with several hotels besides the big one called the "Red Lion." Inevitably, several saloons were established and a newspaper, *The Greenhorn News,* was published every Friday.

TROUBLE OF ALL SORTS, involving shooting scrapes, thefts and holdups plagued Greenhorn in early days. Stout, though tiny jail was built as a consequence, had chastening effect, contained only half dozen tenants during following years. Structure is used now as shelter by deer hunters who cook meals in rock fireplace in front.

A water system was built, possibly unique among mining camps in that every house had its water piped directly to the kitchen. The source was on Vinegar Hill and the water company laid wooden pipes bound with wire to conduct the supply. Everything worked fine, except that elk wallowed in the spring and frequently broke the pipes.

By 1895, some 3,200 people were living their lives in this green wilderness and the nearby forest slopes boasted several large mines besides the Greenhorn, among them the Phoenix, I.X.L., Humbolt and Virginia.

The place had no regular post office until May, 1902, with Burton Miller as first post-master. The town is divided by the line between Grant and Baker Counties, with the post office in the latter. Why postal facilities were not established for so many years after the original gold rush in the 1860's is a mystery.

The Greenhorn Mine was purchased by Richard Baird in 1914 and was operated by him until 1925. Some years after that, with increasing cost of mining and non-advancing price of gold, this and other mines became unprofitable to work and Greenhorn died a slow death.

Its people moved away and many of its buildings fell into decay, to be replaced by the magnificent White Firs, *(Abies Conocolor)*, of the area.

ORIGINAL CLAIM CABIN stands in small clearing. Section marker is visible in front of house. Here in i n f a n t mining camp lived Mr. Carpenter, the first miner to build a permanent home. Staking out homestead claim he did his necessary "improvement work," mined his discovery and built his cabin long before Greenhorn attained its status as town.

BONANZA, OREGON

Frank Roberts was an eager young man when he arrived in the rowdy mining town named after its main mine, the Bonanza. This was in 1900 and he planned to make teaching the mine roughnecks their three R's his work. And he did it, too, for a year or so. He had 25 to 30 scholars of all grades in the tiny Bonanza school.

At that time the big Bonanza mine had been operating since 1877 with a final depth of over 1,200 feet, and a thriving camp had grown up about it. Fifty men were employed in the mine alone and several were required to operate the aerial tram with its 20-to-30-foot towers suspending the cables well above deep winter snows. A constant stream of rich gold ore flowed down this web in buckets to be processed in the 20 stamp mills near the town, giving employment to another 40 or so.

Even this huge capacity could not process the increasing quantities of materials and the mill owners, about 1905, made the bold move of doubling the stamps. This was no simple job in such a remote mountain wilderness.

Pioneer Bonanza teacher, Frank Roberts, is now retired, living in Yamhill, Oregon, but he vividly remembers the various phases of that operation. "The snow was almost gone that spring when those 18 span of horses came up the hill from Whitney. They pulled two large pine logs laid parallel and on them was mounted the boiler necessary to steam power the 20 new stamps. They would come in a rush of 100 feet or so and then have to stop and blow."

During those days anyone could get a job and many did so, for the express purpose of "highgrading," pocketing "blossom rock," ore so heavily laced with gold that its theft paid more than wages. The practice was never wholly controlled and it was felt that many thousands of dollars were lost to the rightful owners this way. Even so, the estimates on total production ran from $1,500,000 to $5,000,000 and it is agreed that the Bonanza was one of the richest in the Baker sector. In addition, extensive placer, sluicing and dredging operations went on in the streams below the town, adding much to the total gained in "hard rock" methods.

Big operations closed down about 1910. Then Frank Dodson and his father took a lease on the property and worked it with more or less success for several years, after which the place died entirely.

MAIN STREET OF BONANZA is lined with ruins. Store on south side, near complete collapse, was center of commercial activity.

WHITNEY, OREGON

Whitney was never a mining camp, though it lived in company with many gold towns. It was strictly a center for logging operations, the surrounding Blue Mountains having heavy stands of Ponderosa Pine and, at higher elevations, Alpine White Fir. The place is wild and wooly, though murders were not as frequent as in some. There *was* a lynching in the spring of 1915 some eight miles south of Whitney. The case involved the rape of a girl and murder of a boy, and the aroused populace had taken justice into its own hands. Law officers, later trying to track down those responsible, met a tight-lipped silence, and soon gave up.

Our same Miss Erma Cole, who figures in our Cornucopia story, taught school in Whitney in the winter of 1919-1920. She had all the children of the first five grades in the tiny schoolhouse on a small knoll near town. Although she started with 28 pupils in the fall and finished with 28 in the spring, only two were continuous, so transient was the logging population.

"I boarded in one of the small hotels near the saloon on the east side of one street," she relates. "The walls were just boards with battens more or less covering the cracks. I had a little sheet iron stove, a bed and a little table for furniture in my 9 x 10 foot room. That winter was extra cold; the thermometer stayed at 55 degrees below zero for a spell, and although the little stove was bright red all the time, I was still cold. When the temperature rose to only 50 degrees below, it seemed almost balmy."

MAIN STREET OF WHITNEY, once thronged with roistering loggers, is now almost silent. Cattle graze in meadow beyond.

HUGE SAWMILL STANDS ROTTING on shore of log pond. Logs were snaked up chute to upper floor to emerge on ground floor at other end as sawn lumber. Spur of narrow gauge ran close by, busily hauled product to all northeastern Oregon.

Each Saturday saw a big dance, and the hotel man made a trip to Prairie City on the narrow gauge earlier each week to replenish his supply of bootleg booze so the festivities would be a success.

That old narrow gauge, the Sumpter Valley Railroad, figures prominently in all the history of our Blue Mountain group of towns. Ahead went the tiny engine, then the little box cars and, trailing behind, a passenger car or two. The trestle crossing a deep canyon between Sumpter and Whitney had a short life, but it is said by the editor of the Sumpter newspaper to have been the second highest in the world, surpassed only by one in the Bavarian Alps. Due to its impressive height it was too shaky and dangerous and was removed in 1915; the grade run around the mountain instead. The little station in Whitney was a neat, well-kept building.

A nearly level meadow is centered by the weathered buildings that are Whitney now. There is no school, depot, hotel or saloon, but a dozen or so residences remain scattered along the main street. Here and there are the ties of the little railroad. At the south end of town is a really imposing sawmill, or the shell of one, the height of a three-story building. A large log pond adjoins it.

EXCEPT FOR HAY, crops did poorly in Whitney. Summers were too short, frosts came late in spring, early in fall, sometimes in August. Machinery stands long idle, rusting away in barnyard.

KITCHEN DOOR and woodshed of old house in Whitney afford study in wood textures.

THE ROLL CALL OF THE SHADOWS

INDEX AND ROSTER OF KNOWN GHOST TOWNS

Publisher's note: This listing makes no pretence of being complete. As this is being written both Mr. Florin and Dr. Mason are in the field photographing and researching the material for additional works to supplement this first volume.

Towns with page numbers are treated in this book, the others listed in small type are candidates for future publications and are listed for the benefit of the reader who may wish to investigate them himself.

NEVADA

Austin	98
Belmont	105
Calico	136
Candelaria	114
Dayton	111
Eureka	97
Fairview	112
Galena	96
Gold Point	117
Goldfield	118
Goodsprings	134
Hamilton	100
Manhattan	103
Midas	94
Nelson	133
Pine Grove	143
Rhyolite	119
Rochester	93
Tonopah	107
Tuscarora	94
Unionville	90
Virginia City	108

Aurora, Bannock, Berlin, Brokenhills, Cortez, Crescent, Delmar, Diamondville, Empire City, Fletcher, Gilbert, Hardin, Ione, Jarbridge, Jessup, Johnnie, Kingston, Leadville, Marietta, Metropolis, National, Ophir, Osceola, Palisade, Queen City, Rabbithole, Rosebud, Tybo, Union, Ward.

NEW MEXICO

Albemarle, Alma, Altos, Baldy, Bonito City, Cabezon, Cerrillos, Elizabethtown, Faywood, Georgetown, Golden, Hillsboro, Hopewell, Kelly, Kingston, Lake Valley, Madrid, Mogollon, Organ, Park City, Pinos Altos, San Marcial, San Pedro, Shakespeare, Terrero, Tyrone, White Oaks.

OREGON

Antelope	154
Austin	167
Bonanza	171
Bourne	164
Cornucopia	159
Granite	163
Grandview	158
Greenhorn	169
Hardman	150
Hoskins	147
Jacksonville	145
Kerby	149
Marysville	165
Shaniko	152
Sumpter	166
Whitney	172

Applegate, Ashwood, Aumsville, Bohemia, Cablecove, Canyon City, Galena, Halls, Maxwell, Minto, Mist, Music, New Era, Pacific City, Promise, Quartzville, Sodaville, St. Louis, Susanville, Willow.

SOUTH DAKOTA

Central City, Cheyenne, Dumont, Galena, Hanna, Hill City, Moon, Rochford, Rockerville, Roubad, Tinton, Trojan.

UTAH

Alta, Bingham Canyon, Copperton, Eureka, Fairfield, Hanna, Jericho, Mammoth, Mercury, Ophir, Park City, Tablona, Tintie.

WASHINGTON

Blewett Pass	29
Copper City	23
Index	24
Liberty	30
Skamokawa	18
Sultan	25
Trinity	26
Wilkeson	31

Aegenas, Ardenvoir, Conconully, Dyer, Galena, Garland Springs, Holden, Mineral City, Monitor, Monte Cristo, Northport, Republic, Ruby, Silverton, Synarep.

WYOMING

Atlantic City	74
Diamondville	70
South Pass City	72

Battle, Dennison, Dillon, Dines, Duncan, Du Noir, Elkhorn, Encampment, Gold Hill, Lenore, Merna, Miner's Delight, Rambler, Viola.